Jaime J. Sucher

Shih Tzu

Everything About Purchase, Care,
Nutrition, Behavior, and Training

BARRON'S

CONTENTS

What Is a Shih Tzu?	5

Humans and Dogs	5
Origins and Early History	5
Characteristics of the Breed	7
Deviations from the Standard	9

Should You Buy a Shih Tzu?	11

An Intelligent Choice	11
Adult or Puppy?	13
Male or Female?	14
Buying a Shih Tzu	15
Selecting a Puppy	17
Bringing Your Puppy Home	18
Expenses	18

Housing and Supplies	21

Indoor Requirements	21
The Great Outdoors	24
Additional Accessories	25
Dog Toys	27

Caring for a Shih Tzu	31

Preparations	31
Adjustment	32
Lifting and Carrying	35
Shih Tzu and Children	35
Vacation Time	36
Boarding	37
Pet Sitters	37
HOW-TO: Grooming	38

What Do I Feed My Dog?	41

What Is High-Quality Dog Food?	42
Feeding Table Scraps	43
How Many Meals Do I Feed My Shih Tzu?	44
The Importance of Water	44
Does My Shih Tzu Need Nutritional Supplements?	44
Special Considerations in Feeding Your Shih Tzu	44

Ailments and Illnesses	47

Choosing a Veterinarian	47
What Are Symptoms?	48
Immunization: The Pros and Cons	49
Infectious Diseases and Vaccines	50
Of Worms and Worming	51
External Parasites	52
Common and Hereditary Ailments	55
Skeletal Disorders	56
Other Disorders	59
Home Care for the Older Shih Tzu	63
When It Is Time to Say Good-bye	66

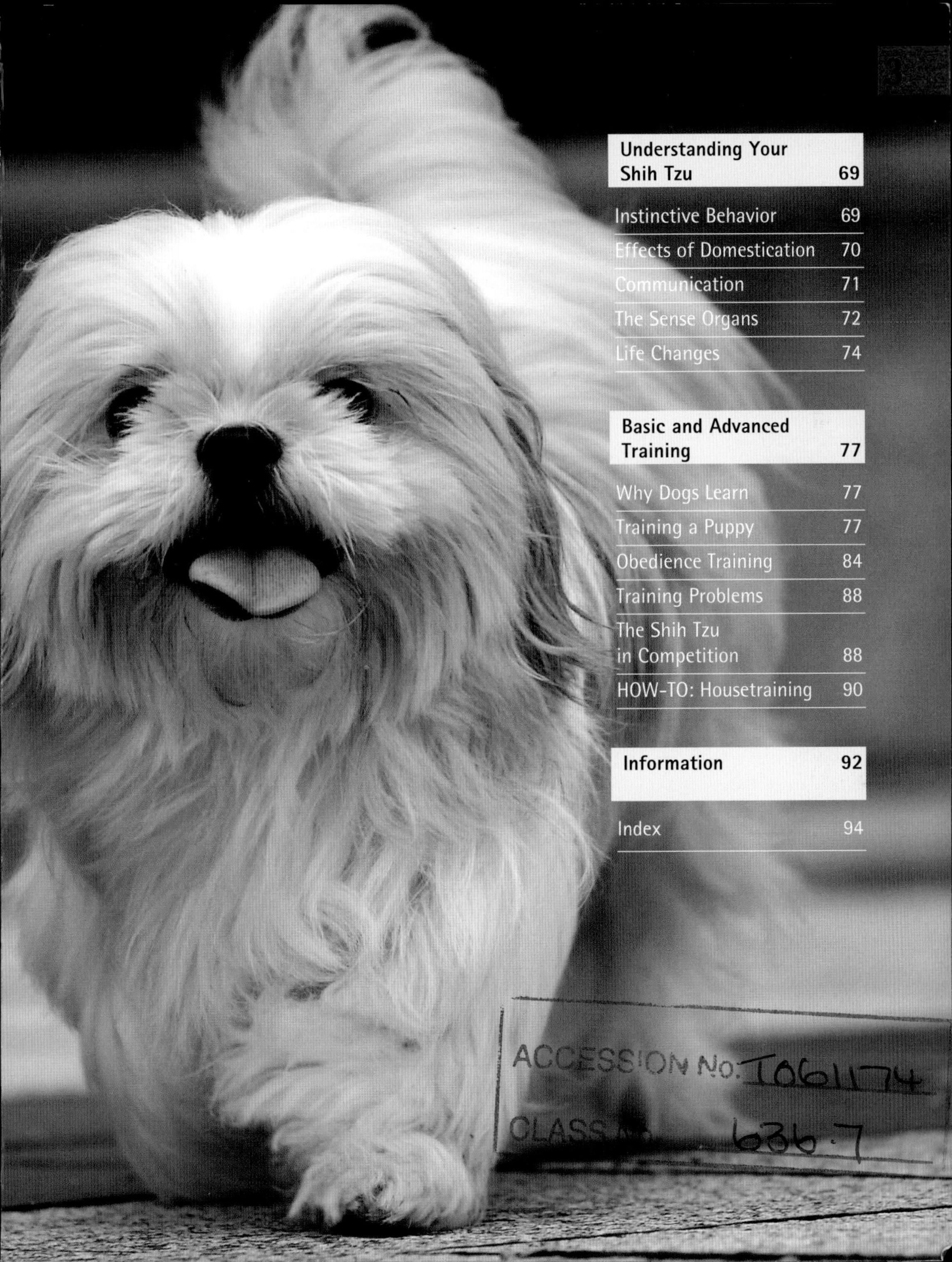

**Understanding Your
Shih Tzu** 69

Instinctive Behavior 69

Effects of Domestication 70

Communication 71

The Sense Organs 72

Life Changes 74

**Basic and Advanced
Training** 77

Why Dogs Learn 77

Training a Puppy 77

Obedience Training 84

Training Problems 88

The Shih Tzu
in Competition 88

HOW-TO: Housetraining 90

Information 92

Index 94

WHAT IS A SHIH TZU?

Dogs are considered the first domesticated animals. The actual domestication process is hard to trace because it is impossible for archeologists to distinguish tame wolves from early domestic dogs. They agree, however, that the earliest indisputable records of "dog" remains date back more than 12,000 years.

Humans and Dogs

Long ago, our ancestors learned how to domesticate wolves, and as a result, this wonderful creature that we call dog has become a part of our culture. At first, the dog was valued as a hunter; as time went on their immense loyalty made them valued protectors of human life, property, flocks, and herds. Although in modern times we may still use them as hunters, herders, and protectors, our relationship with dogs has gone well beyond that of owner and worker. Dogs have become our dearest companions and our favorite pets.

The toy-dog group can be considered the furthest extension of our emotional ties to dogs. Unlike other breeds that were originally bred to tend sheep, retrieve fallen prey, or rescue injured people, toy dogs were developed strictly for pleasure. Although some of them do make excellent watchdogs, these dogs were created simply to be house pets and companions.

Origins and Early History

The exact origins of the Shih Tzu (pronounced Sheed-zoo) are really unknown, but there is enough evidence available to create a theory that most experts think is accurate. There are documents, paintings, and other art objects of Chinese origin that contain references to images of a form of dog believed to be the original ancestor of the modern Shih Tzu. The oldest document dates back to the Tang dynasty, in the year A.D. 624. It says that a pair of these dogs was given to the royal court by a Chinese nobleman. It is believed that the nobleman obtained the dogs from the ancient empire of Byzantium. Unfortunately there is little further documentation for the 370 years that followed. The next mention of these dogs (or a breed that was very similar) comes in the years A.D. 990–994. when the people of the Ho Chou province gave a pair to the Imperial Court as a tribute. It is believed that the dogs were later bred in the Forbidden City of Peking for several centuries.

Later records written during the Manchu dynasty of the mid-seventeenth century claimed that early relatives of the Lhasa Apso were brought from Tibet to the Forbidden City. The highly prized Apsos were sometimes given as gifts by the Dalai Lama of Tibet, or may have been taken by Manchu generals as spoils of war. Such dogs were placed at the feet of the emperor as a sign of fealty, or as a symbol of conquest. It is believed that these Tibetan Apsos were bred with the native dogs of the Chinese royal palace.

The original ancestors may have been a relative of the Chinese Pekingese, or at least, at one point in time, there were some crosses with this breed. It is also believed that in the Imperial Palace there were some crosses with a smooth-coated breed that was the ancestor of the modern Pug. Whether these crosses were intentional or not, they definitely played an important part in the origins of our modern Shih Tzu.

There are several pictures of a small, lion-faced (i.e., the lion as depicted in traditional Asian art) dog that appear in the Imperial Dog Book of the Manchu Dynasty, and there are records indicating that these special dogs were selected with great care for court breeding. From these came the Shih Tzu that we know today. Although the word *Shih Tzu* is Chinese for "lion dog," they were often referred to as a chrysanthemum-faced dog. One look at a Shih Tzu groomed in the traditional Chinese manner will tell you why. This method consists of combing out the dog's mustache and beard away from the face, and roughing up the hair behind the head and on the shoulders to form a large, puffed-up head of fur that resembles the aforementioned flower.

The writings in the Imperial Dog Book tell of how these small, intelligent, and docile dogs were bred by court eunuchs. They would compete with each other to produce specimens for the emperor. If a dog caught the emperor's eye, a picture of it would be placed in the court record book, which was considered a very great honor.

It is known that the Shih Tzu was a highly favored house pet of the royal family for well over 200 years. Unfortunately many dogs were destroyed during the Revolution because they were viewed as a symbol of imperial rule. Only a few of the royal dogs escaped.

In 1930, Lady Brownrigg, an Englishwoman living in China, was able to save a pair of Shih Tzu and import them to England. Their names were Hibou (the male) and Shu-Ssa. Shortly afterward, another male, named Lung-Fu-Ssu, was imported into Ireland. Later in the 1930s a few more Shih Tzu were saved by an English officer on duty in China. All of the Shih Tzu we know of today are descendants of these dogs. In 1934, the Shih Tzu Club of England was formed, and the first championship awards were given in 1940.

From England, the breed spread to Scandinavia, to other European countries, and to Australia. During World War II, members of the armed forces stationed in England were introduced to the breed, and later brought a few back to the United States. It was not until 1950 that a considerable number of Shih Tzu were brought into this country. Not only did they come from England, but a large number also came from France, Denmark, and Sweden.

The Shih Tzu was recognized as a separate breed by the American Kennel Club (AKC) in 1955. Once recognized, they were allowed to be shown in the Miscellaneous Class, which no longer exists. In 1957, the Shih Tzu Club of America was formed, and in 1963 it merged with the Texas Shih Tzu Club, to form the American Shih Tzu Club (ASTC). The Shih Tzu was admitted registration to the AKC Stud Book in March 1969 and obtained its regular show classification in the Toy Group in September 1969.

As you can see, the Shih Tzu has only a short history outside of China. Shih Tzu were not known to the Western world before 1930 because it was literally impossible to obtain one during the reign of the Chinese emperors. These dogs were the personal property of the royal family, and anyone who attempted to acquire one illegally was usually put to death. Since 1930, however, this favorite breed of the royal Chinese courts has quickly spread in popularity.

In 1952, an intentional cross breeding of the Shih Tzu with a Pekingese took place in England. This was done because there were so few Shih Tzu in Great Britain that some breeders thought there was a danger of the dogs becoming seriously inbred. Many Shih Tzu at this time were suffering from poor bone structure, poor pigmentation, and pinched nostrils. It was felt that a cross with a Pekingese would help reduce these problems and, at the same time, would not alter any of the other traits that characterize the breed.

In 1957, the English Kennel Club introduced a rule that allowed all Shih Tzu that were four generations removed from the Pekingese cross to compete as pure Shih Tzu. The AKC, however, was not nearly as lenient. They would not recognize any dog that did not have a ten-generation purebred Shih Tzu pedigree. Since then, there have been no further crosses, and all of the purebred Shih Tzu of today are more than ten generations removed from the Pekingese cross.

Characteristics of the Breed

The following descriptions are an interpretation of the AKC-approved Shih Tzu Standard. The standard is a complete written description of the breed; how it should look, act, and move. You can obtain a copy of the written Standard from the ASTC or the AKC.

General Appearance: The Shih Tzu should be sturdy, lively, and alert, with a long, flowing double coat. Because of its noble heritage as the palace pet of several Chinese dynasties, the Shih Tzu has a "distinctively arrogant carriage." The Shih Tzu will move with its head held high and its tail curved over its back. Although a certain amount of variation in size is accepted, the Shih Tzu must be "compact, solid, carrying good weight and substance."

Size, proportion, substance: The Shih Tzu should have a height at the withers (the highest point of the shoulders) of between 8 and 11 inches (20-28 cm). Mature dogs should weigh between 9 and 16 pounds (4-7 kg). The length of the Shih Tzu, from the withers to the base of the tail, should be slightly longer than its height at the withers. It should not appear either "leggy" or "dumpy or squatty."

Head: The head of the Shih Tzu should be round, broad, and wide between the eyes, and the top of the head must be domed. The head must be in proportion to the rest of the body, and appear neither too large nor too small. The facial expression will impart a "warm, sweet, wide-eyed, friendly, and trusting" feeling. An overall well-balanced expression is more important than any individual part.

Eyes: The eyes must be large, round, placed well apart, and look straight ahead; however, they should not be too prominent. They should be very dark in color, but, on liver- and blue-coated dogs, the eyes may be lighter.

Ears: The proper Shih Tzu ears should be large, heavily coated, and slightly below crown of the domed skull.

Muzzle: The muzzle must be set no lower than the bottom rim of the eye. It should be square, short, and smooth, and must never be downturned. The overall length of the muzzle should be no more than 1 inch (2.5 cm) from the tip of the nose to the stop (the base of the forehead). The length will vary in proportion to the overall size of the dog. The front of the muzzle should be flat. The lower lip and chin should not be protruding or receding. The jaw is broad and wide, and its bite should be undershot. The teeth and tongue should be hidden when the mouth is closed.

Nose: The nose, like the lips and eye rims, is black (except on liver-pigmented dogs, where it should be liver-colored, and on blue-pigmented dogs, where it should be blue). A Shih Tzu's nostrils are broad, wide and open.

Neck, topline, and body: Once again, the overall balance is most important. The neck should be sturdy and flow smoothly into the shoulders. Its length should allow the dog to hold its head high, and should be in proportion to the height and length of the dog. Its back should be level and parallel to the ground. The body is short and sturdy, and there should be no evidence of a waistline or tucked-in abdomen. The body should be slightly longer than the tail. Shih Tzu possess a broad and deep chest with good rib spring. They should not, however, be barrel-chested. The depth of the rib cage should extend to just below the elbow. The distance from the elbows to the withers is slightly longer than from the elbows to the ground. The croup (the highest part of the rump) should be flat.

Tail: The tail is set high on the hindquarters and is heavily "plumed." It should be carried in a curve well over the back.

Forequarters: The shoulders are laid back, well angulated, laid in, and fit smoothly into the body. The forelegs are straight, muscular, and firmly attached to the body. Because of the broad chest, they should be set well apart; however, the elbows must be close to the body. The pasterns (the equivalent of a forearm) are strong and perpendicular to the ground. The feet of a Shih Tzu are firm, and well padded and point straight ahead.

Hindquarters: The angle and position of the hindquarters should be in balance with the forequarters. The rear legs, like the forelegs, are well-boned and muscular. When viewed from the rear, with the stifles (the equivalent of the human knee) well bent, the legs should be straight and not too close together, but still in line with the forelegs. The hocks (the next joint below the stifle) are perpendicular to the ground. The rear feet are firm, padded, and pointed straight forward.

Coat: A Shih Tzu's double coat is long, luxurious, thick, and flowing and at times may have a slight wave.

Gait: This breed should move straight, and at its natural speed should display "smooth, flowing and effortless movement." The dog should demonstrate a good reach and equally strong rear drive. Its back should remain level during movement, and its head should be carried high. Even when moving, the tail should remain curved over the back.

Temperament: Because the sole purpose of a Shih Tzu is to be a companion and house pet, the Standard dictates that it is essential that its temperament be "outgoing, happy, affectionate, friendly, and trusting towards all."

Deviations from the Standard

The Breed Standard is used by judges to determine a dog's faults in the show ring.

If you are interested in getting a prospective show dog, I highly recommend that you obtain a copy of the Standard and become extremely familiar with it. For those who are seeking a home companion and do not intend to show their dogs, physical faults, such as too long or too short legs, a narrow head, and so on, should not be a major (or even a minor) concern. What should be important to all prospective Shih Tzu owners is to always consider the dog's temperament. Hostility, nervousness, shyness, and lack of vitality or self-confidence are all undesirable traits in a Shih Tzu, and may indicate other problems (both mentally and physically). So whether you are seeking a top ring performer or a loving home companion, be sure that the dog's temperament is what it should be before making your selection.

SHOULD YOU BUY A SHIH TZU?

As a companion dog the Shih Tzu has some excellent credentials. It was the favorite house pet of the royal family in imperial China, and shortly after its introduction into England it became the dog of choice for many lords and ladies, including the Countess of Essex.

An Intelligent Choice

The same virtues that have made this breed the choice of royalty have likewise been the reason for the Shih Tzu's recent increase in popularity. The diminutive size that characterizes the breed makes it the ideal choice for urban life. It makes an excellent apartment dog, especially for someone who is living alone or without children. This is a breed that cannot live alone in kennels, but flourishes in the society of human beings.

The Shih Tzu is a small, compact breed. It is also very hardy and sound. It is a long-haired breed, whose coat comes in a wide variety of colors and patterns. Underneath all its hair, the Shih Tzu hides large, drooping ears, short legs, a broad, sturdy body, and a short muzzle.

The Shih Tzu is a lively and vivacious dog. It is intelligent, very alert, and possesses a good temperament. Like many of the toy breeds, Shih Tzu are proud, have a keen sense of themselves, and at times can be extremely self-centered. I have heard those who are not familiar with the breed describe them as "haughty" or even "arrogant," but Shih Tzu owners like to refer to their dog's personality as "totally human," and count this as a major reason for the breed's success.

If you are considering the purchase of a Shih Tzu, you should think your decision over very carefully; owning any dog is a responsibility that should not be taken lightly. There are all too many people who have rashly purchased a dog without being aware of, or prepared for, the needs of the animal. The result of these impulsive acts is usually an unhappy owner and an equally sad dog. So before you go out and get yourself a dog, review the "Considerations

CHECKLIST

Considerations Before Buying

1. Do you have, or plan on having, small children in your home? The Shih Tzu can be a poor choice as a pet for a new and growing family. Like many other toy breeds, they are very possessive of their owners, and may become jealous of a small child and vie for attention. In addition, the breed's small size does not allow her to stand up physically to the rough-and-tumble abuse she can receive from a rambunctious child.

2. Are you the nervous type or easily excitable? The Shih Tzu is a very active and alert dog, and can become excited very easily. During these times they may run around and bark a lot. Although these are good watchdog qualities, they may be upsetting to some people.

3. Do you have the time, patience, and energy needed to properly raise a dog? The long coat of the Shih Tzu requires daily grooming, and puppies need to be trained and housetrained.

4. Are you willing to devote some of your free time to the dog? Shih Tzu require

significant human companionship for their emotional well-being. If you travel a lot, or take long vacations away from home, you must be willing to either take the dog with you or find a sitter for your pet.

5. Do you intend to keep your dog in an outdoor kennel? The Shih Tzu is a house-dog, and must be kept indoors. Although she will need to go outdoors to do her business and get some exercise, you must not expose this breed to harsh weather for a prolonged period of time. Shih Tzu are not very tolerant of cold weather.

6. Do you understand the long-term commitment of owning a Shih Tzu? A dog may live with you for as long as a child and will likely spend more time at home. The life span of this breed is ordinarily 13–14 years, and is sometimes longer.

7. Can you afford to keep a Shih Tzu? In addition to the initial purchase price, you will need to buy supplies. Food alone can cost as much as $40 to $50 per month. You will also have to pay for those annual visits to the veterinarian.

Before Buying" list, and answer the questions openly and honestly. The answers will let you know if you are ready to own a Shih Tzu.

As the owner of a dog, you are responsible for her in every way. A dog's health and soundness are dependent upon its owner feeding her properly and giving her all the medical care she needs. Also, the way your dog behaves

depends on how well you train her. As you can see, there is much to consider before you buy a Shih Tzu.

If you need answers to any other questions, or if you wish to talk to a local breeder before making your decision, contact the American Shih Tzu Club (ASTC). (For address see Information, page 92.) They can supply you with a list of registered breeders and the address of the nearest chapter of the ASTC.

Adult or Puppy?

There is little question as to why four out of every five people desiring to purchase a dog begin by looking for a puppy rather than an adult dog. Just one look at a litter of Shih Tzu puppies will tell you why. How can anyone resist wanting one after they see those tiny, clumsy balls of fur frolicking with their littermates in such a carefree manner? A single glimpse can melt the coldest heart.

Indeed, one of the greatest pleasures of owning a Shih Tzu puppy is to watch her grow from this small, delicate bundle of energy into a proud, dignified, and intelligent member of the family. This, however, takes a lot of patience, time, and energy. Puppies need constant care. They must be fed more frequently and watched more carefully than adult dogs, and need to be housetrained.

For those who cannot give a puppy all that she needs, choosing an adult would be much more advantageous. By getting an adult dog, you can free yourself from the drudgeries of housetraining chores and rigorous feeding schedules. The adult Shih Tzu would also be a benefit to anyone who does not have enough flexibility in their daily schedule to accommodate a puppy's needs.

An adult Shih Tzu will usually adapt easily to a new owner and environment, and would make an ideal pet for the elderly, or anyone else for whom raising a puppy would be too much work. The greatest drawback to buying

TIP

Rescue Organizations

Consider working with a Shih Tzu rescue organization. These nonprofit groups are dedicated to finding people who can provide a caring, loving home for abandoned, abused, or unwanted dogs. Rescue groups can be found on the Internet or through the ASTC.

These organizations are a great source of information, and will provide sound advice before, during, and after an adoption. They will also make sure that the dogs they put up for adoption are up-to-date on vaccinations and are spayed (if old enough). Rescue groups are committed to finding the right match for their dogs, so you have a better chance of getting a dog that is right for your lifestyle. As these organizations are not always privy to a dog's history, they take extra time to understand a dog's temperament and match it to prospective owners. In this way they spend more time finding the right home for their dogs, and less going through the rescue process for a second time.

an adult Shih Tzu is that it may be difficult to correct any bad habits that she may have previously acquired.

The choice, then, is evenly divided between obtaining an older dog that would doubtless be easier to care for, or getting a puppy and raising her to adapt to one's own lifestyle. If you are looking to obtain a show dog, however, the choice may become one of monetary feasibility.

There is a certain amount of luck involved in buying a potential show puppy. While you can check the puppy's lineage, and you can see the conformation of the dam (mother), you cannot be sure that the puppy will grow up with the desired looks and temperament. In fact, the Shih Tzu does not reach full maturity or beauty until the age of almost three years. On the other hand, if you wish to purchase a proven adult show dog, it will cost a significantly greater amount of money.

Male or Female?

Another choice you will have to make when choosing your Shih Tzu is whether to get a male or a female. This is usually an easier choice, for it is more a matter of personal preference. In Shih Tzu, there are only slight differences in the temperaments of males and females. Females are usually more even-tempered except when they are in season, while males may become more irritable from time to time. There is little difference when it comes to training, although females do tend to be slightly friendlier, while males will be more ruggedly independent. These differences are so slight that unless you have raised both sexes simultaneously you might not even notice them.

Where the choice of male or female becomes more important, however, is if you decide that you want to raise puppies. If you are considering starting a kennel, then you would want a female. If you plan to buy a second Shih Tzu and you already have a male, sometimes bringing a second male home may lead to fights (although bringing home a female may lead to other obvious problems). If you have a female you can get another female without worries.

If you select a female and have no intention of breeding her, then have her spayed. There is an alarming number of unwanted and homeless dogs in the United States, and every precaution a dog owner can take to prevent unwanted pregnancies should be taken. The spayed female is also less likely to suffer from breast tumors, ovarian cysts, false pregnancies, and other ailments. Likewise, male dogs should be neutered. Neutered males are less likely to develop testicular or prostate cancer.

If you plan on entering a conformation dog show, do not have your dog spayed or neutered because it will be immediately disqualified.

Buying a Shih Tzu

If you wish to buy a high-quality Shih Tzu, it is of the utmost importance that you deal with a well-established and reputable source. You can get a list of reliable Shih Tzu breeders in your area from the American Kennel Club or the secretary of the American Shih Tzu Club, or from your local Shih Tzu club. You can also perform a Web search for Shih Tzu, but you should never buy a dog on-line, as the Internet is full of people who would not hesitate to mislead and take advantage of unwary buyers. Instead, use it to find breeders to add to your list of kennels to visit.

When visiting each breeder, you should inspect their dogs and the conditions in which

they are kept. While it will be difficult to walk away from the first cuddly, furry puppies you see, it is advisable to visit as many breeders as possible, regardless of the distance. It is extremely important to obtain a healthy and well-cared-for puppy. A sickly, poorly raised puppy may need extensive medical care, and may not properly develop physically and/or emotionally. By finding the right dog at the beginning, you can save yourself a great deal of effort, money, and heartbreak later on.

During your inspection, make sure that the premises in which the puppies are kept are clean and that the puppies have an ample amount of room to move about. Watch the puppies interact with each other to see if they seem happy and healthy. Observe the coat condition and overall appearance of the puppies and the mother. These are all indicators of the quality of the operation.

In the world of dogs, one finds that the highest-quality pets are offered by the best and most conscientious breeders. They are, therefore, usually more expensive. Never be tempted to buy a "cheap" dog. Shih Tzu that are offered at bargain prices are usually no bargain at all. It is more than likely that there is something wrong with them. These dogs may be in poor health, or may have been raised strictly for profit by an inexperienced or unscrupulous breeder.

So take your time. Talk to all the breeders in detail. Be thorough in your investigation of their premises and breeding stock. Most breeders will even give you the names of others who have bought Shih Tzu from them. Call these references to see if they are satisfied. Then, once you are confident in your choice of breeder, it is time to select a puppy that will suit your purposes and fit in with your lifestyle.

Selecting a Puppy

Choosing a Shih Tzu puppy that is to become a house pet and member of your family is much different from selecting a potential show dog. In either case, emphasis should be placed on the overall health of the puppy.

A healthy puppy will have a clean, smooth, and shiny coat. Its ears should be clean of any type of discharge. The puppy's eyes should be clear and bright. Feel the puppy's body and legs. You should feel the solidity of the body muscles and the strong leg bones. Lift the puppy's hair and examine its skin. It should be moist and smooth, and free from flakes or scales. You should also examine the condition of the puppy's mother.

Check the pedigree of their breeding stock. Ask if their medical history includes the results of Orthopedic Foundation for Animal evaluations for hip and elbow dysplasia, which are hereditary joint formation ailments. Also, because the Shih Tzu is prone to several hereditary eye diseases, be sure the breeder's stock have received eye clearance tests from the Canine Eye Registry Foundation. If the breeder does not have his/her dogs tested, then you should ask why.

Once you feel confident about the health of the puppies and the quality of the breeder, it is time to choose the right puppy for you. If you are looking strictly for a family pet, then it becomes a matter of personal choice where the temperament and color or markings of a particular puppy catch your fancy.

If you are looking for a potential show puppy, then you should be concerned with more than just the puppy's health. One of the keys to selecting a potential show dog is examining the puppy's pedigree papers. These papers are a written record of the dog's more recent ancestry, and indicate all show champions in its lineage. Although there is no guarantee that a puppy who is a descendent of championship stock will also be a winner, the odds will at least be better than if you obtained a puppy that has no proven ancestry.

If the puppy's pedigree and health are satisfactory, then you should look for a puppy with the proper show temperament. Shih Tzu that are exhibited in dog shows should be active, alert, and carry themselves with the distinctive arrogance that characterizes the breed.

Once you have selected your Shih Tzu, ask the breeder for the date the puppy was wormed, and be sure to get a written record for your veterinarian of this and any vaccinations she may have received. Never be afraid to ask breeders questions. A good breeder is just as concerned as you are about making sure his or her puppies get the best treatment. Always keep a line of communication open.

When you finally complete the purchase of your new Shih Tzu puppy you should receive her AKC registration certificate (or an application form to fill out), her pedigree papers, and a health certificate from the breeder's veterinarian. If the puppy has already received her formal registered show name from her breeder, then you should complete the transfer by sending the registration certificate (AKC papers) and the appropriate fee to the American Kennel Club. After they complete the transfer of ownership to you, they will send you a new certificate. If the puppy has not been named, then you will complete the application, choose the dog's formal name, and send it with the fee to the AKC.

Bringing Your Puppy Home

As a general rule, the earlier you can bring your new puppy home, the easier it will be for her to adapt to her new environment. Also, the younger the puppy, the less likely the chances of her picking up any bad habits that the new owner may find hard to break. On the other hand, the puppy must be old enough to eat and drink on her own.

The optimum age at which a Shih Tzu puppy should be brought into her new home is seven to eight weeks. An eight-week-old puppy should have little trouble adapting to her new environment. Recent studies have indicated that puppies are very sensitive to changes in their surroundings during their eighth to ninth week. By placing a puppy in her new home at seven weeks, you can avoid any undue stress or behavioral problems that may occur. These studies also suggest that if you cannot bring the puppy home earlier, then it would be best to wait until the ninth week.

Expenses

The purchase price of a top-quality Shih Tzu will vary; however, you should expect to pay at least $400. Naturally, puppies from champion-caliber parents may sell for $1,200 or more. In general, the younger the dog, the less expensive she is because the breeder has invested less time and money in her.

As stated earlier, food may cost as much as $40 a month. You will also need to purchase special equipment for feeding, housing, and grooming your new dog. Your Shih Tzu will require immunizations against all infectious diseases, and additional veterinary costs may occur if your dog gets sick or injured.

In many townships there are fees that must be paid in order to obtain a license for your dog. There are also the fees you will have to pay to register your dog with the American Kennel Club, as well as the annual dues should you decide to join the Shih Tzu Club of America.

As you can see, the costs of owning a Shih Tzu go far beyond the initial purchase price. Consider this carefully before deciding to buy.

HOUSING AND SUPPLIES

The Shih Tzu does not require large amounts of room like many of the large breeds; however, it is important to their mental and physical health that they have a protected feeding and sleeping area, where they can eat in peace and seek refuge whenever the need arises.

Indoor Requirements

As previously mentioned, the Shih Tzu is considered a house dog. Therefore, the majority of her life will be spent indoors. The small size of this breed allows the Shih Tzu to adapt to life in a city apartment just as easily as it would in a big country home.

Keep in mind, however, that dogs are territorial animals and their behavior and mental well-being are greatly affected by their environment. Making sure that your Shih Tzu has the proper indoor space requirements is the first step in assuring the proper adjustment of your pet to its new environment. Dogs that are subject to cramped living quarters, or are not given an area where they can sleep undisturbed, can become stressed and nervous. This in turn can lead to changes in biological functions, including digestive and excretory problems.

While most indoor dogs are allowed to have the run of the house, it is important that your Shih Tzu be given two special areas in your home in which it will remain relatively undisturbed. These are her eating and sleeping areas.

Your Shih Tzu's eating area should be located in an easy-to-clean part of your home. Rooms that have tile or linoleum floors, such as a kitchen or bathroom, are usually the best. Once this location is chosen it should not be changed. If you do not have any rooms in your home with an easy-to-clean floor, you can buy a small piece of linoleum and place it under your dog's food dishes. The location of the food and water dishes should allow your Shih Tzu to eat in peace. If you put the dishes near a wall or in a corner, away from frequently traveled paths, it will give the dog the peace it needs to eat and digest its meals properly.

The sleeping area, like the feeding area, should be placed to allow your Shih Tzu to sleep or rest without being disturbed. The best sleeping areas are in the corners of rooms that are not subject to heavy human traffic. Corners are good because they offer your dog protec-

CHECKLIST

Rules of Puppy Safety

Before bringing your new puppy home, review the following rules with your family and friends. In addition to preventing injury, these rules will help your puppy feel comfortable and safe in her new home and help increase her confidence in you and your family.

1. Avoid unnecessary excitement. Let the puppy adjust to her new surroundings.

2. Prohibit rough play. Puppies are very fragile creatures and should be handled with care.

3. Avoid picking up the puppy too much. Let her do her own walking as much as possible. This will allow her to get her exercise and to improve her motor skills.

4. Be sure everyone in your household knows the proper way to lift and carry your puppy. The proper technique is described in detail later in this chapter.

5. Do not subject your puppy to unnecessary heights because of the risk of falling. When it is necessary to place the puppy on an elevated surface, such as when you are examining or grooming her, someone must be present the entire time to ensure the puppy's safety.

6. Do not give bones or other hard objects to a young puppy. Until a puppy reaches about six months of age, she has only her milk teeth and cannot chew hard objects.

7. Try not to leave the puppy unsupervised during the first few weeks.

tion on two sides, creating a more comfortable and secure feeling. The corner you choose should be draft-free and have direct sunlight.

Try to select an area that will make it easy for you to confine your dog's movements. When you are away from home, or when you go to sleep, you may wish to prevent your Shih Tzu from having access to the entire house. In these cases, your dog will need to be confined to a part of your home that will give her free access to her eating and sleeping areas.

The temperature of your Shih Tzu's sleeping area is also important. An adult Shih Tzu needs the sleeping area to be kept about 70°F (21°C), while a puppy requires a warmer climate of about 75°F (24°C). Puppies are more susceptible to catching colds, so the sleeping area should be located away from heat sources, and not subject to excessive increases or decreases in temperature.

Your Shih Tzu's sleeping area should be equipped with either a sleeping box and pad or a crate with a pad. Although you should make this choice in advance, I recommend using a crate because of its many benefits.

Before domestication, dogs were cave-dwelling animals. Instinctively, the modern dog finds security in any cave-like structure, once familiar with it. If you choose a crate, you will find that your dog will actually prefer to sleep there and will return on her own. The crate can also be used as a housetraining aid (see the chapter entitled Basic and Advanced Training), for traveling, and can also prove useful, for short periods, when you are unable to supervise your puppy. Fiberglass travel crates are ideal (provided they are of suitable size), as their construction is extra rugged and they are easy to clean.

The crate should be approximately 18 inches (46 cm) high, by 18 inches wide, by 24 inches (61 cm) long. The welds should be strong enough to resist the efforts of an active puppy. Should you choose to use a crate, it will also act as the puppy's house when you are not around to supervise her. The crate thereby needs to be large enough to house your Shih Tzu, yet easy to handle when you travel.

If you decide not to use a crate, then you will need a sleeping box. The box should be large enough to accommodate a full-grown, stretched-out dog. Place a plastic liner and some newspaper on the bottom of the box (just in case of accidents) and an old blanket or pad on top.

If you decide to purchase a sleeping box, avoid those made of wicker or soft wood. An active Shih Tzu puppy, despite her small size, is capable of chewing them apart. Likewise, avoid boxes that are painted or stained. Many of these coatings are toxic, so unless you are absolutely positive about the harmlessness of the materials used, it is better to be safe than sorry. If you decide to build your own sleeping box, then the same rules apply. Use only nonsplintering hardwoods, and avoid using any paints or stains.

It is extremely important to keep your dog's sleeping area clean, especially if you have a puppy. Puppies have a low resistance to disease because their immune system is not fully developed. Everything you put into your puppy's sleeping box should be clean.

The Great Outdoors

Shih Tzu are house pets and should never be left outdoors for a long time. As a matter of fact, the only time your Shih Tzu needs to be outside is during exercise periods or when she has to do her "business." Even at these times, your dog should be closely supervised.

Unless you have a fenced-in yard that is Shih Tzu-proof, your dog should be on a leash when she is outdoors. If you do have a fenced-in yard, and you wish to allow your dog to run free, you should still take your Shih Tzu for walks and allow her to relieve herself

away from your property. If not, your dog may feel that she can relieve herself any place she chooses, and before long your entire yard can become quite messy and full of unpleasant odors. Your Shih Tzu will also appreciate her yard being kept clean. It is equally important that your Shih Tzu learns to behave just as well outdoors as she does indoors.

Under no circumstances should you consider keeping your Shih Tzu in an outdoor doghouse or a confining run. Generations upon generations of Shih Tzu have been bred to be companion animals. Much of their character and personality has been shaped by their heritage as house pets. If your Shih Tzu is to develop into the mature, self-confident dog that she is intended to be, she will need to be raised indoors, like any other member of your family.

During the cold winter months, the outdoor activity of your dog should be limited to your routine walks. While the Shih Tzu is a long-haired breed, it does not withstand the cold very well. This breed's undercoat lacks some of the insulating quality of other dogs, especially those of the hunting or working breeds.

Finally, when you take your dog for her leashed walks, remember that you are completely responsible for your dog's actions. Do not allow your pet to wander around the neighbor's garden while you turn your head the other way. After all, nobody wants to wake up and find an unexpected and unwanted present on their lawn. Take your dog to an uninhabited area and allow her to relieve herself. You should also be aware that in many areas it is required by law that you clean up after your dog. Even if you live in an area where it is legal, you should prevent your dog from relieving herself in open and public areas.

Additional Accessories

Bringing home a new Shih Tzu puppy or adult will surely be an exciting and hectic event in any household. In order to prevent any excessive confusion from occurring on the big day, there are a few supplies you should purchase beforehand. Being prepared ahead of time will help you avoid having to make any trips away from home. It is very important that your puppy not be left alone during those first few days when she is adjusting to her new environment.

Among the most important equipment you will need are your dog's food and water dishes. These items come in a variety of sizes and can be made of different materials, which include metal, ceramic, glass, and plastic. When choos-

ing these dishes, keep in mind that a Shih Tzu is a small breed whose head, when standing, is barely inches above the ground. Pick dishes that are not more than 3 inches (7.5 cm) deep. If you are feeding a puppy, you will have to use a very shallow bowl, or even a plate. The idea is to select feeding dishes that will allow your pet free access to her food and water. In addition, the dishes that you choose should be made in such a shape as to prevent tipping. Despite their diminutive size, a Shih Tzu with a voracious appetite may attempt to "wolf down" your culinary concoctions. If the bowls are not tip-proof, it could result in a real mess.

The choice of material from which the dishes are made is really a matter of personal prefer-

ence. The only warnings to be given concern ceramic and plastic bowls. If you buy a ceramic bowl, be sure it is designed for food use. Some ceramic pieces are fired using a lead-based glaze. Bowls that are coated in these materials can result in lead poisoning if they are used over a long period of time. Plastic bowls may leach chemicals into dogs' drinking water, which can be harmful to their health. If you plan to clean your dog's bowls in a dishwasher, make sure they are made of a material that is dishwasher safe.

Two pieces of equipment that you will need when you first go and pick up your Shih Tzu

are a collar and a leash. The Shih Tzu, whether a puppy or an adult, does not require a strong collar made of chain. In fact, they need a lightweight collar, preferably made of nylon or leather. If you look carefully, you should be able to find one that is adjustable enough to fit both a puppy and a full-grown Shih Tzu. During the life of your dog, however, you may have to purchase more than one collar. Both nylon and leather collars will deteriorate with age, so you should check them from time to time. If you choose to use a metal collar, be sure it is not too heavy or too bulky. In addition, this type should only be used on an adult

TIP

Reflective Tape and ID Tags

I recommend using reflective tape (or tags) on both the collar and leash. These will make both you and your dog more visible to car drivers, making your nighttime walks much safer. You should also attach an identity tag to your dog's collar that gives your name, address, and telephone number. This inexpensive tag could prove invaluable should your beloved pet ever become lost.

Shih Tzu, and not a puppy—puppies are not capable of handling the extra weight of a chain collar.

Leashes, like collars, are also made of nylon, leather, or chain. Because you need have little fear of your Shih Tzu's body strength, there is no need for a chain leash at any time (in fact if chewed on, they can damage a puppy's teeth). You can find an adequately strong leather or nylon leash in just about all sizes.

There are several types of leashes available, and the styles you choose are dependent upon your intended uses. For regular walks, you need a leash that is only a few feet long. Never use an extremely long leash when you are out for a stroll. A short leash will enable you to bring the dog to your side quickly should the need arise. If you give the dog any extra leeway when you are out for a walk, you are only asking for trouble. There is always the chance of your dog bolting into a busy street, and if you are using an extra-long leash, you may

be helpless to prevent a tragedy. If you wish to restrict the movements of your Shih Tzu, a 30-foot (10-m) leash with an automatic reel may prove useful.

Another item you should have for safety reasons is a muzzle. In all my years as a dog owner, I am thankful that I have never had to use a muzzle, but I still keep one in a handy spot, just in case. Muzzles can be very helpful in handling an injured dog. Any dog, regardless of its size, may act unpredictably when it is in severe pain. If you must take a dog that is seriously hurt to the veterinarian, a muzzle can be a good precaution. When buying a muzzle, make sure that it can be adjusted for size to fit both an adult and a puppy. If you are planning to take your dog abroad, you may have to get a muzzle because some foreign countries require that all dogs wear them.

As a dog owner, it is almost inevitable that you will eventually have to deal with the problem of external parasites. You should therefore keep a pair of tweezers and some rubbing alcohol on hand, to remove ticks properly, and disinfect the wound.

Dog Toys

While most dogs are supplied with adequate toys, most owners fail to understand their importance in maintaining both the physical and psychological well-being of their pets. Dogs, especially puppies, like children, need toys. Toys prevent your dog's life from becoming too tedious. Toys mean playtime! They let your puppy know that there is more to life than eating, sleeping, and training. Giving your Shih Tzu a toy will allow her to work out and burn up extra energy, thus giving the

SAFETY TIP

Choosing Safe Pet Toys

Because a puppy's teeth are sharp, you will need to keep a close eye on her toys. Rawhide and nylon chew toys must be replaced before they become small enough to swallow whole. Avoid soft toys that can be shredded and swallowed by an active dog. Swallowing large or foreign objects can cause choking or a blockage of the dog's digestive system.

Be sure all of your Shih Tzu's "chew" toys are designed for dogs and made of nontoxic materials. Remember that many forms of plastic are toxic, and soft woods tend to splinter. To be safe, avoid all painted or varnished toys, as these can contain chemicals that are harmful to your pet. Finally, monitor your dog's toys and discard any that start to break into pieces or fray.

potential prey. They will attempt to track them down. They will try to sneak around behind their prey and crouch, waiting until the moment is right. Finally the puppy will attack. If all goes right, your puppy will render the toy harmless, and carry it around, victorious. Once this is done, your Shih Tzu may repeat the act all over again. Even hundreds of years of domestication are not enough to rid your dog of this instinctive behavior.

Should you still doubt the importance of dog toys, there is one other good reason to use them. Shih Tzu puppies are energetic and industrious little bundles of mischief. One way or the other, your puppy will find something to play with. If it is not a chew toy, then it might be the slender leg of your new coffee table. If it is not a tennis ball, then it might be your fuzzy slippers. If it is not a squeaky toy, then it might be your checkbook.

From the time a puppy begins to teethe until she reaches a ripe old age, she should always have a chewable toy to gnaw on. The

dog some of the exercise she needs. Toys also allow your dog to relieve any frustrations that may have been building.

Dog toys will also help your puppy sharpen her survival instincts. Some dogs treat their toys as if they were

best types of chew toys are nylon or rawhide bones. As your puppy gnaws, the rawhide becomes soft enough to prevent damage to the teeth. At the same time, this helps to strengthen your Shih Tzu's jaw muscles. Make sure you get a bone small enough for your puppy to handle properly.

Incidentally, not all dog toys have to be store bought. Tennis balls, although too large for your Shih Tzu to get in her mouth, can still be pushed and rolled around. An empty cardboard box can be the source of much fun and adventure for a curious puppy. Feel free to be creative, but remember to use your common sense as well. Do not allow your Shih Tzu to play with anything small enough to swallow, or made from any material that she can pulverize.

As a final thought on dog toys, I will resort to a story as told to me by a friend. It seems that my friend had just purchased a new puppy (although not a Shih Tzu), and had been acclimating her to life in her new environment. One day, in his attempts to keep his new little friend entertained, he got an old slipper from his closet and began a game of tug-of-war. As it turned out, the dog became very fond of that slipper and of playing their new game. Unfortunately, the puppy's newfound fondness for footwear did not stop there. One day upon returning home from a long day's work, my friend found himself in need of a new wardrobe of footwear. Almost every shoe, sneaker, or slipper that carried his scent had been thoroughly chewed or slobbered upon. The moral of this story is to be selective about the items you give to your puppy to use as toys. To a Shih Tzu puppy, there is little difference between your old slippers and your new ones. This goes for any object that may carry your scent.

CARING FOR A SHIH TZU

It is inevitable that your first days home with your new puppy will be rather hectic. Luckily, there are things you can do to reduce the stress on both you and your new housemate.

Preparations

In addition to purchasing your equipment and supplies in advance, there are other ways of preparing yourself and your home in order to make your puppy's transition easier. Aside from the food and water dishes, collar, leash, toys, and bedding supplies, you will also need the proper grooming supplies. (These will be explained later in this chapter.) In addition, you will also want to pick up an adequate supply of puppy food. Use the same food that your puppy's breeder used. Changing the puppy's food during this emotional time increases the chances of dietary upsets.

Once this is done, it is time to puppy-proof your home. Puppy-proofing is the act of taking all potential hazards in your home and putting them out of the puppy's reach. Remove all potentially harmful chemicals, including paints, cleaners, pesticides, and disinfectants. Store these in an area that is inaccessible to the puppy.

You must also remove all sharp objects such as nails and staples. If you own an older home, make sure you remove all flaking paint or paint chips. Older paints contain lead that, if ingested, can be harmful to both humans and animals.

Finally, all electrical wires should be moved out of your puppy's reach. A dog that chews on electrical wires can be injured or killed by the resulting shock. If you are in doubt as to whether or not an object is within your dog's reach, it would be best to move the object and not take any chances. Remember that puppies are very curious creatures. They will roam through a house and explore every last inch that they can possibly get to. A puppy will sniff, paw, and attempt to chew on almost everything she encounters. In addition, do not take the small size of your Shih Tzu puppy for granted. She will use her lack of stature to her advantage by getting into every nook and cranny she can find.

Adjustment

It is inevitable that your puppy will experience a certain amount of loneliness during her first few days in your home. Prior to moving, the puppy felt safe and secure with her brothers and sisters, knowing that her mother's watchful eyes were always upon her. Now she is alone in a strange world that is full of unusual sights and sounds. This type of stress would affect anyone, let alone a tiny, defenseless, and very impressionable seven-week-old puppy.

Make your puppy's first day in her new home a quiet one. Let her know she is entering a calm, safe, and secure environment. Speak to your new friend in a soft, reassuring tone. Let her know that there is nothing to fear, that she will be taken care of. The last thing your puppy needs is to be placed in a strange new world and then be confronted by a mob of poking, prodding humanity. So put off introducing your new puppy to your friends for a few days.

Ideally you will be able to pick up your puppy yourself. When you pick up your Shih Tzu, find out from the breeder when her next feeding is, and how much food you should give her. While you are returning home, speak softly to your puppy, allowing her to become accustomed to the sound of your voice. From the first moment you have the puppy, you should begin calling her by her given name.

When you arrive home, take your puppy for a walk. She will probably want to urinate or defecate. Take her to the area that you have chosen to be her elimination area, and allow her to do her business. Give her plenty of time to relieve herself, for most puppies will want to explore for a while. After she is finished, be sure to pet and praise your puppy. You might as well start your outdoor puppy training right from the beginning. When all is done, it is time to go indoors.

Once inside, remove your puppy's leash, and allow her to explore your home undisturbed. Every five or ten minutes you can approach the puppy and speak to her. Feel free to pet her gently, but do not force the puppy to do what she does not want to do. In time, the sound of your footsteps and these brief approaches will quickly wear away any insecurity and ease the feeling of loneliness. After an hour or two, introduce your new puppy to the location of her food and water dishes (if she has not found them already) and feed her if necessary.

By the time you bring your Shih Tzu puppy home she should be fully weaned and able to feed on her own. When feeding your puppy, you will need to follow three fundamental rules. First, as already mentioned, feed your puppy the same type of food as the breeder used. Second, continue to follow the same feeding schedule as the breeder. Should the feeding times prove inconvenient, you can slowly change the meal times to suit your needs. Third, never bother your dog while she is eating or sleeping. Dogs that are surprised can act unpredictably and might snap at you. This is a very important rule to relay to your children.

T I P

Feeding

1. At first, keep the puppy on the same diet it was receiving from the breeder to minimize digestive system stress. If you want to change the puppy's diet, do it gradually by mixing into the diet larger amounts of the new food while reducing the old food proportionately.
2. Try to feed your puppy on the same schedule as the breeder. However, if that is inconvenient, gradually shift the feeding times to meet your schedule.
3. From the start, try removing your puppy's food from her (while she is eating) for a few minutes, and then return it to her to continue eating. If you do this regularly, it will reinforce your position as "master" over your dog (which is critical to successful dog training).
4. Never surprise your dog while she is eating (or sleeping). A surprised dog may act unpredictably, so be sure to explain this rule to everyone else in your household as well.

After feeding the puppy, take her outside for another walk so she can relieve herself. On returning, let the puppy roam freely, but feel free to pet her and play with her. Once the puppy begins to tire, pick her up and place her in her sleeping box or cage. After a few days, your puppy will learn where her sleeping area is and when she is tired, will find her bed on her own.

The First Night

Chances are that the first night your puppy is in your home will not be pleasant for anyone concerned. You and your family will encounter your first real test of dog ownership, and it is of the utmost importance that you pass.

It is more than likely that on this first night your puppy will begin to whine, whimper, and wail, because she feels lonely and misses her mother and siblings.

When your puppy looks tired, put her in her bed with a few toys. Draw the curtains and turn out the lights to make the room as dark as possible. Then leave the room, making sure that the puppy cannot get out and cannot hear or see you. Most likely she will begin to cry. If this happens, wait at least five minutes before returning. Should the puppy settle down, let at least ten minutes pass before reentering the

TIP

Sleeping

It is extremely important that your puppy learn to sleep alone in her own bed. If the puppy whines, pick her up and quickly bring her to a previously chosen outdoor elimination spot and place her on the ground. When she has urinated or defecated, praise her, pick her up, and return her to the crate. You should then return immediately to your own bed. If the puppy does not "go" after a sufficient time has passed, return her to her crate, and return to your bed. If the whining continues, try sitting next to your puppy's bed, calming her with soothing words or petting her, but do not pick her up and comfort her. The puppy needs to learn how to behave when she is alone, and it is best to start this lesson as soon as possible. As soon as she calms down, go back to your own bed.

room. Repeating this procedure throughout the day will help lessen the feelings of isolation and alienation that your puppy will experience at night.

Home Alone

If it is at all possible, do not leave your puppy alone for long periods of time for the first few days. In addition to the emotional stress being left alone can cause your puppy, the amount of trouble an unsupervised curious puppy can get into is mind-boggling. If you must leave, have a relative or close friend "puppy-sit," preferably in your home. Taking your puppy to another new place will only lead to more anxiety.

After a few weeks, when your Shih Tzu has begun to feel completely comfortable in her new home and has gained your trust and confidence, you can leave her alone for longer and longer periods. Regardless of your confidence, however, I urge you to limit your puppy's access to the portion of your home that contains her eating and sleeping areas. Also be sure to inspect these rooms again to ensure that no potential hazards are within your puppy's reach.

Lifting and Carrying

Learning to lift and carry your Shih Tzu puppy properly can prevent the pain and possible injury that improper handling can cause. This is an important lesson for every member of your family to learn, and is really very easy. A healthy adult Shih Tzu will weigh only about 10 or 11 pounds (4.5–5.0 kg) so she can easily be lifted by most people in the same fashion as a puppy.

Place one hand under the puppy's chest and support the rump and hind legs with the other. That is all there is to it. This hold should give you a firm grip on your puppy, and make it difficult for her to squirm, which might cause you to drop her. Never pick up your puppy by placing only one hand under her abdomen, and never grab the puppy by her legs. These methods can hurt the puppy. You should also forget that classic image of grabbing your puppy by the scruff of her neck. Besides being humiliating, it also hurts.

Shih Tzu and Children

While it may seem logical to get a toy dog such as a Shih Tzu for a young child, in reality this is not the best thing to do. This does not mean that in some instances children and Shih Tzu do not hit it off. It is just that Shih Tzu are not capable of withstanding the rough-and-tumble play that some children will dish out.

While Shih Tzu are naturally loving and affectionate, they may at times become intolerant of competing against children to gain your attention. Older children, however, and those who are more introspective, will more than likely form a lifetime relationship with a Shih Tzu. If you have an older, considerate child who would be willing to spend some time taking care of a Shih Tzu, there is no reason to believe that they cannot live in perfect harmony. However, if you have a more typical young child, you are well advised not to introduce a dog into your family that may not want to share the spotlight. If you do have young children and somehow come into possession of a Shih Tzu, you must instill in the youngsters the proper way to handle and play with the dog.

It would also be good to get the children involved in the responsibilities of dog ownership. Have your children feed, groom, and take your Shih Tzu for walks. In this way you can help build a bond between them that will lead to a long and lasting relationship.

Vacation Time

Vacationing with your Shih Tzu can be a fun and rewarding experience for both of you. All it takes is a little advance planning. Not all airlines, cruise ships, and trains accept dogs, and many have significant restrictions. For example, some airlines will transport dogs only when the temperatures are not too cold or too hot

at both ends of the flight, and some will not let dogs travel in the passenger cabin, only the cargo hold, so be sure to read all the rules on the carrier's website.

In the United States federal law requires that dogs traveling by air must be certified by a veterinarian within ten days of the flight to be healthy, vaccinated, and free from contagious diseases. You may also have to deal with security. When you check in your baggage, you will also need to check in your dog. To do this you will need to remove the dog from her travel crate, which is put onto a conveyor belt and goes through the X-ray check, and have your dog walk with you through the metal detectors (so be sure to remove any metal ID tags).

If you are traveling by car, you can place your Shih Tzu in her crate. Do not allow the dog to run free in the car. There are usually enough problems on the road to deal with; you don't need the additional worry about what

your Shih Tzu is doing. When driving, open the window enough to give your dog fresh air, but do not expose her to drafts. Drafts can lead to ear, eye, and throat ailments. Make rest stops about every two hours. During these breaks, take the dog for a walk and allow her to relieve herself. Needless to say, walk the dog on a leash. You should also give your dog a drink of cool water. It can get very hot inside a car, and frequent drinks will help to prevent dehydration.

Many young dogs may become carsick if they are not used to traveling. Your veterinarian can supply you with motion-sickness tablets to prevent this.

If you are traveling abroad, obtain a copy of the rules pertaining to pets from the consulate of the countries you are visiting. Some countries have the same requirements as domestic trips, and some have special quarantine regulations. To visit most foreign countries your dog will require a valid health certificate, which you can get from a licensed veterinarian. You will also need a current certificate of vaccination against rabies.

When you pack your dog's suitcase, remember to bring the following items: food and water dishes, collar, leash, muzzle, crate with blanket, and grooming equipment. If it is at all possible, bring enough of your dog's regular canned and/or dry food to last the entire trip.

Boarding

If you cannot find a reliable neighbor, friend, or family member willing to dog-sit, then you must consider boarding your Shih Tzu. Start by contacting the breeder from whom you purchased your dog. If it is not possible to

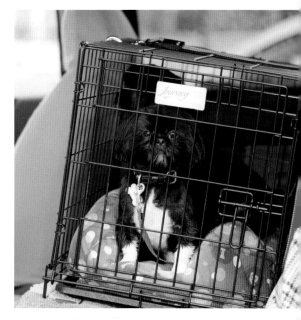

leave your dog with the breeder, then you may decide to use a boarding kennel.

Before leaving your dog at a boarding kennel, you should inspect the facilities thoroughly. Make sure they are clean and that the operating staff is knowledgeable. An adult Shih Tzu should have little problem adjusting to a temporary change in her environment. If it can be avoided, however, a Shih Tzu puppy should never be left alone or at a boarding kennel for a long period of time.

Pet Sitters

Another great alternative is to keep your Shih Tzu at home and hire a pet sitter to check in on your pet throughout the day. You can check your phone book or the Internet for a professional pet sitter near you, or ask your veterinarian or friends for referrals.

If you brush your dog daily, it should take only a few minutes. Aside from this, your Shih Tzu will only require additional grooming periodically.

To make the grooming easier, I recommend acclimating your dog to these sessions while she is still a puppy.

Equipment

To keep your Shih Tzu in top show condition, you will need the following equipment: a brush with flexible pins, a slicker brush, a comb, scissors, and nail clippers designed for dogs. Another handy item is a tangle-removing spray, formulated for dogs.

Coat Care

A Shih Tzu's coat is much easier to brush if misted with water or tangle remover. If the coat is matted, remove all matting with a slicker brush before you wet the dog. Water tends to set in matted hair, making it almost impossible to remove without cutting it out. After you dampen the coat, you can brush it until it is dry, then apply more spray if needed. Light daily brushings and a thorough weekly brushing will prevent unmanageable matting.

When brushing, begin with the chest, underside, and inner legs. Place the dog on her back, spray the exposed coat, and brush lightly with a pin brush. Make a part in the dog's coat and brush it in layers, starting at the skin and stroking toward the tips. When you are done with the stomach and chest, use the slicker brush to fluff up the coat around the feet and legs.

Turn the dog onto each side so you can do the heavy coat on the side of the hocks and body. Again spray, part the hairs, and brush in layers from the skin to the tips. Once all is completed, the dog should be allowed to lie right side up. Spray, and then part her coat down the middle from the nose to the base of the tail.

Brush the long outer coat and then comb it out until smooth; then spray and brush out the dog's tail. The final step is to carefully smooth out the dog's whiskers and the hair around the face and eyes using a fine-tooth comb.

Part of your normal routine should be to trim any excess hair between the dog's toes as short as possible. This can help reduce the chance of infection in bad weather and can improve traction.

If you wish, you can tie up the hair on the top of the Shih Tzu's head. Once the grooming session is over, reward your dog with a kind word, some affectionate petting, and a few minutes of play.

Always look for signs of parasites when grooming your dog. If you see signs of fleas or ticks, address the problem immediately. Contact your veterinarian if you notice anything unusual.

Bathing

Unless your dog smells bad, is totally filthy, has gotten covered with something greasy, or is about to be enter a show ring, you should not bathe your dog. Unlike human skin, a dog's skin is full of oil glands, which help keep the skin soft and prevent it from becoming dry and cracked.

They also secrete an oil that helps the dog's coat repel water. Excessive use of any soap or shampoo will remove the oil produced by these glands and dry out the skin or cause excessive shedding.

When a bath is absolutely necessary, you should start by brushing your dog to remove tangles. Use a high-quality shampoo designed especially for dogs, and avoid getting shampoo or water in your dog's ears or eyes. After shampooing, thoroughly rinse out the coat. When the bath is finished, gently pat the dog dry with a towel. Let your pet shake several times, and then wrap her in a towel and blot dry. Then comb and part the dog's hair. Keep the dog indoors during the drying process. A Shih Tzu should be dried with a blow dryer; one with a stand will free both your hands to work on the dog. Brush the dog gently while her coat dries to separate the hair and speed up the drying process.

Ear and Eye Care

During your thorough weekly grooming session, give special attention to your Shih Tzu's ears. Use a commercial ear-cleaning solution to carefully remove any wax build-up. To clean the ear, hold it open with one hand and gently clean the inside of the flap with a cotton swab dipped in cleaning solution. Use a fresh cotton swab for each ear. You can also clean the outermost portions of the ear canal using cotton swabs.

Also, inspect your Shih Tzu's eyes regularly to ensure they are free of discharge. Use a moistened cotton swab to remove any dirt around your dog's eyes. Again, use a fresh swab for each eye. If you notice any damage or inflammation, contact your veterinarian.

Nail and Paw Care

Learn how to use a pair of clippers before you trim your dog's nails. An experienced dog

When trimming your Shih Tzu's nails, be sure to clip them at an angle. Be careful not to cut the sensitive quick.

groomer or veterinarian can show you how to use them. The center of the dog's nail is called the quick, and it contains the blood vessels and nerve endings. You can see them when you examine the dog's nails (it is normally a pink to deeper red color). If you cut the quick, you will cause the dog much pain. In addition, the quick grows out as the nail lengthens. If you wait too long between pedicures, you may have to cut the quick to get the nail back to a comfortable length. Always cut the nail as close to the quick as possible, and be sure to hold your pet's paw firmly but gently.

Tooth Care

Tooth care begins with feeding your dog plenty of hard foods, such as dog biscuits and nylon or rawhide bones, to slow down the accumulation of tartar. Excessive tartar can lead to gum deterioration and tooth loss. You should also brush your dog's teeth once a week with a commercial toothpaste that is formulated specifically for dogs. Before brushing, inspect the dog's teeth and gums for signs of infection and tartar buildup. Excessive tartar can be scraped off by your veterinarian.

WHAT DO I FEED MY DOG?

The nutritional requirements of dogs have probably not changed very much from the time they were first domesticated. Our understanding of those needs, however, has increased greatly in recent years.

The National Research Council (NRC), a division of the National Academy of Science of the United States, has interpreted vast quantities of data and published a study titled "The Nutritional Requirements of Dogs." This study established the minimum amount of every nutrient (protein, fat, carbohydrates, vitamins, minerals, and trace elements) needed to maintain the health of the average middle-aged and older dog, as well as growing puppies.

The NRC study serves as a guideline for all companies that manufacture commercial dog food in the United States, to help them formulate their products. In fact, for a dog food to be certified as "complete and balanced" in the Unites States, it must meet or exceed all of the nutritional requirements established by the NRC. In addition, it must pass actual feeding tests as established by the Association of American Feed Control Officials (AAFCO).

Although their ancestors (wolves) are scientifically classified as carnivores, modern domestic dogs have evolved to a point where they can effectively use a wide variety of foods to meet their nutritional needs and therefore are considered omnivores. This allows modern commercial dog food manufacturers to use a wide variety of ingredients to achieve the mandated nutritional profiles. Unfortunately for the consumer, that can make it very hard to determine which dog food is best for your Shih Tzu. To help decide, seek the advice of your breeder and veterinarian. Breeders will know what food works best on their Shih Tzus, and veterinarians have a working knowledge of dog foods based on the experiences of other clients. A veterinarian will also be able to recommend a special diet should your pet's health dictate the need for one.

I strongly urge all dog owners to use a high-quality commercial dog food rather than

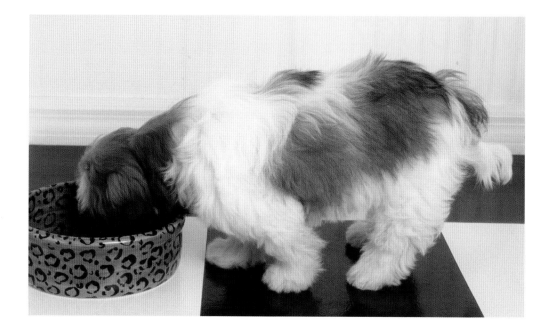

preparing their pet's food from scratch. When preparing meals at home, it can be difficult to determine if you are giving your loving companion too much or too little of an essential nutrient. It is also significantly more expensive and much more time consuming (time you can use playing and exercising with your beloved pet). If, however, you feel that, as an act of love, you want to prepare your dog's food fresh, then I strongly advise you to read as many books as you can on animal nutrition and seek the advice of your veterinarian.

What Is High-Quality Dog Food?

Like human food recipes, the ingredients used to make commercial dog foods have varying degrees of nutritional value. Most "complete diets" are supplemented with a sufficient quantity of vitamins and minerals, but the ingredients used in a high-quality dog food should also be easily digestible and free of chemical additives, which over the long term can have harmful effects on your pet.

When looking for a high-quality diet, check the label to make sure the pet food was tested using AAFCO procedures and is complete and balanced. This statement can be found at the end of the nutritional information panel.

Check the ingredients listing. By law, the label must contain a list of ingredients, with the most abundant ingredient (by percent weight) listed first and continuing in descending order. The primary ingredients listed in a high-quality dog food should be easily recognizable, such as chicken, beef, lamb, brown rice, carrots, and peas. Ingredients such as

The Basic Nutrient Groups

Nutrient (Sources)	*Nutritional Value and Symptoms of Deficiencies*
Protein (meat, eggs, fish, milk, soybean meal, brewer's yeast, wheat germ)	Provides energy and amino acids essential for growth, development, maintenance of strong bones, and muscles; promotes production of antibodies, enzymes, and hormones; deficiencies include poor growth, weight loss, loss of appetite, and poor hair and coat.
Fats (meat, vegetable oils)	Provide source of energy and heat; supply essential fatty acids, fat soluble vitamins (A, D, E, and K); make food more palatable; necessary for proper development of skin and coat; deficiencies include dry and coarse coat and skin lesions.
Carbohydrates (sugars, starches)	Help regulate energy balance; supply fiber and roughage to help regulate digestive system and help prevent diarrhea/constipation.
Vitamins (brewer's yeast, vegetables, fruits, cod liver oil, wheat germ oil)	Prevent numerous illnesses and diseases; help regulate many bodily functions including growth, muscle development, and fertility; deficiencies can lead to skin lesions, depression, conjunctivitis, nervous disorders, rickets, and osteoporosis (as well as numerous other disorders).
Minerals/Trace Minerals (bones, meat, grains, fruit, vegetables)	Prevent numerous ailments and diseases; help regulate many bodily functions including bone formation; help regulate water balance within a dog's body. (Trace minerals are named because they are required in very small quantities.)

cornmeal, wheat, soy, and white rice are carbohydrate fillers that are not easy to digest and provide little nutritional value. Be extra cautious with wheat- and soy- based products, as they are both allergens, and Shih Tzus tend to be more prone than many breeds to food allergies. Look for foods that use meat meals, rather than animal "by-products." Meat meal is actually meat with the water removed, whereas "by-products" contain the indigestible parts of animals, including feet, feathers, hooves, and hair. Finally, avoid foods that contain chemical antioxidants such as BHA and BHT. High-quality dog food will instead use vitamin C or vitamin E to prevent fats from turning rancid.

Feeding Table Scraps

Many people think they are obliged as loving pet owners to feed their precious pooches leftovers. Be warned that this practice has great potential for teaching your Shih Tzu really bad habits, such as begging. In addition, feeding the wrong table scraps to your dog can lead to obesity, which in turn can lead to health issues later on. I have also seen where this practice can lead to dogs refusing to eat their regular diet, which can also result in problems related to improper diet or malnutrition.

How Many Meals Do I Feed My Shih Tzu?

Relative to their body weight, a Shih Tzu can eat larger quantities of food than humans at a single meal, so they do not need to be fed as frequently. Adults can be fed one or two times a day. Puppies, however, need to be fed more often. A puppy between four weeks and three months old needs to be fed at least four times a day. Because dogs react well to routines, you should create a feeding schedule and stick with it. A good time to feed your dog is during the family meals, so she is occupied while the rest of the family is at the dinner table.

The Importance of Water

Of all the nutrients in a dog's diet, there is none more important than water. Water is vital to every living cell and comprises nearly 60 percent of your dog's body weight. Unlike some animals, dogs cannot store much water and must constantly replenish whatever they lose. This means that you must make sure your dog has an adequate supply of water at all times. A Shih Tzu's water intake will depend on several factors, including air temperature, the type of food she eats, the amount of exercise she gets, and her temperament. Be sure to avoid giving your dog very cold water, especially after exercise or if she is showing signs of heatstroke. Cooling the dog's body down too fast can be counterproductive and lead to other severe illnesses.

Does My Shih Tzu Need Nutritional Supplements?

This is a very controversial topic at the moment. Although there is plenty of information available, it is often difficult to separate the information that comes from the manufacturers of nutritional supplements from that of independent researchers.

Naturally, the manufacturers of these items are interested in selling their products, but getting too much of some nutrients (such as vitamin D) can be toxic and have dangerous side effects. The amount of nutrients your Shih Tzu needs will depend on several factors, including diet, age, activity level, medical conditions, and environmental stresses. This means that not all dogs need nutritional supplements, whereas some may have very specific needs. Before you give your dog any supplement, particularly vitamins or minerals, you should consult with your veterinarian. He or she will review with you the critical factors affecting your dog's nutritional requirements before giving you advice.

Special Considerations in Feeding Your Shih Tzu

Although the National Research Council provides the minimum nutritional requirements for puppies, adult, and older dogs, several other factors affect the type and quantity of food an individual dog needs. Growing puppies require about twice the amount of calories per pound of body weight as a middle-aged adult, and older dogs require about 20 percent less than an average adult.

As a result, puppies need special diets that are higher in proteins and fats to support their growth and metabolic needs, and older dogs, with their slower metabolism, can become over-weight if their diet is not changed. Exercise and environment will also influence the quantity of food your Shih Tzu needs.

The best indicators that your companion is getting the proper amount of nutrition are her body weight and coat condition. Your dog is at an ideal weight if you can feel her ribs and can easily discern the waist from the ribs when running your hands down the side of her body. You should also be able to feel the abdomen slightly tucked up. If you have an underweight Shih Tzu, you will easily feel her ribs, vertebrae, and pelvic bones, and you will not feel any fat on the bones. Severely malnourished dogs lose muscle mass, and puppies will have stunted growth. When a Shih Tzu is overweight, you cannot feel the ribs and may see fat bulges over her back. In addition, the waist will not be discernable from the ribs and the abdomen will drop.

A dry coat and flaky skin may signify a fat, fatty acid, or vitamin deficiency. This condition is often accompanied by scratching and is many times misdiagnosed by pet owners as external parasites or other skin ailments. The proper diet should produce a soft and shiny coat that is rich in color.

A Final Note

You should know that dogs do not require a wide variety of foods and will not tire from eating the same thing every day. If you feed your Shih Tzu a high-quality, well-balanced diet, she can thrive on that food for most of her life. If your dog is not eating properly, it may be an indicator of a physical or emotional problem. If your Shih Tzu falls off her diet for a day or two, there may not be any reason to worry and the dog's appetite may return on its own. But if your dog refuses to eat for more than two days, it may be a sign of a serious problem and she should be taken to the veterinarian for an examination.

AILMENTS AND ILLNESSES

Dogs, like humans, are subject to a wide variety of illnesses. Although the Shih Tzu is no exception, you will be glad to know that there are several things you can do to prevent many of the ailments described in this chapter.

Proper nutrition, good hygiene, and an adequate exercise program are essential in keeping your Shih Tzu healthy. By providing these requirements, combined with scheduled visits to the veterinarian, you can help your pet to live a long and healthy life. You must never underestimate the importance of keeping scheduled appointments with your veterinarian. Early detection is the key to preventing many problems from getting out of hand, and it sometimes takes a trained medical eye to detect early symptoms.

Choosing a Veterinarian

The worst time to look for a veterinarian is when you really need one, so make sure you have chosen your veterinarian before you bring your new Shih Tzu home. When looking for a veterinarian, keep in mind that you are looking for more than a medical expert. You are looking for someone to meet the needs of both you and your pet; someone with "people" as well as "animal" skills.

Like your doctor, veterinarians often work with a staff of professionals (technicians, administrators, and aides) so you will likely want to evaluate the competence and caring of the entire team. Location, fees, facility cleanliness and suitability are also very important factors that you will need to evaluate. Weigh all of the issues that are important to you, but remember that you will probably be happier if you drive a few extra miles or pay a few extra dollars to get the care you want for your companion.

The best way to find a good veterinarian is to ask people who have the same approach to pet care as you. Look for recommendations from friends, breeders, animal shelters, dog trainers, groomers, and pet sitters. Once you have narrowed your search, schedule a visit to meet the staff, tour the facility, and learn about the veterinary philosophy on treatment and the hospital philosophy.

Once you think you have completed your research, it is time to make your choice. Only you can determine what factors are the most important, but under no circumstances should this decision ever be made by cost alone.

What Are Symptoms?

Simply put, symptoms are indicators of diseases or disorders, and because dogs cannot talk, symptoms provide the only signs that your pet is not feeling well. Although understanding the symptoms, or combinations of symptoms, associated with certain ailments may help you narrow down the possibilities, the trained eye of a veterinarian is usually required to determine the exact cause of your Shih Tzu's illnesses or ailments.

Symptoms to Watch For

There are several symptoms of which every dog owner should be aware. If you notice any one, or combination of them, you should call your veterinarian. Be alert for the following:

- exhaustion
- loss of appetite or thirst
- excessive appetite or thirst
- unusual sneezing or wheezing
- excessive coughing
- runny nose
- discharge from the eyes or ears
- poor coat condition
- foul breath
- blood in the stool
- slight paralysis
- limping, trembling, or shaking
- swelling or lumps on the body
- sudden weight loss
- cloudy or orange-colored urine
- inability to urinate
- uncontrolled urination
- moaning or whimpering
- unusual slobbering or salivation
- vomiting
- diarrhea

The last two, vomiting and diarrhea, are probably the most common of all canine symptoms; however, they do not always indicate the presence of a serious ailment. For example, young dogs sometimes wolf down their food with such speed that their natural defensive mechanisms send it right back up again. It is also common to see a dog eat grass and subsequently vomit in a voluntary attempt to purge the digestive tract. This behavior is completely natural, and may not necessarily be an indicator that a larger problem exists. Persistent vomiting, however, can indicate a very serious ailment and should be reported to your veterinarian immediately. It can be caused by several digestive disorders and diseases and is often accompanied by irregular bowel movements, including diarrhea.

Likewise, the occasional soft stool is usually nothing to worry about. During the warmer summer months, dogs tend to drink more water, and as a result, their stools may become loose or they may even have diarrhea. Short-term acute diarrhea can also be caused by minor stomach upsets. Acute diarrhea starts suddenly and lasts for a few days to a week. Most cases of acute diarrhea can be handled at home, by changing your dog's diet. Try using a diet consisting of half boiled rice and half cooked chicken. Do not restrict your dog's water intake when she has diarrhea, and be sure to keep offering her a clean, fresh supply.

Chronic diarrhea (continuous or frequent watery bowel movements, where your dog is acting sick during the worst bouts), on the other hand, can indicate a serious problem.

Longstanding diarrhea can become a severely debilitating disorder. It can cause your dog's body to lose valuable nutrients and its ability to detoxify properly, and impair her immune system functions. This can lead to the development of secondary disorders and will become even harder to treat. Whenever you see the signs of chronic diarrhea, you need to bring it to the immediate attention of your veterinarian.

Immunization: The Pros and Cons

Before the discovery of vaccines, several infectious diseases ran rampant through the canine population, leading to a large number of deaths. Fortunately, advances in modern medical science led to the development of vaccines that can protect dogs against the bacteria and viruses that cause most major infectious diseases. Although all vaccines are extremely effective, not all are needed by every dog and not all offer permanent protection.

For years the standard practice was to give dogs scheduled booster shots and, in some cases, the frequency with which they were given was determined by local law. This "better safe than sorry" practice is now the topic of heavy debate. Homeopaths have long argued against frequent vaccination, claiming that vaccines are not as benign as first believed and that dogs that are vaccinated excessively or needlessly are subject to more diseases and disorders than dogs that are not. In reaction to this, many veterinary schools have begun researching the effects of vaccines, to determine if their effect on the long-term health of the dog outweighs the benefits gained from the currently recommended vaccination protocol.

Another approach being used to determine the need to revaccinate is called *titer* testing.

This test is used to determine the levels of specific disease-fighting antibodies the dog has in her bloodstream. If the titer test reveals sufficient levels of a specific disease-fighting antibody, it is a good indicator that the dog has immunity against the disease and that revaccination is not needed. Unfortunately, a low or absent titer does not always indicate that the dog does not have immunity.

A dog's immune system has a "memory" and will not expend energy developing unnecessary antibodies if it has the ability to produce more within a day or two of exposure to an infectious organism. So even though titer testing will tell if a dog has a level of antibody to give her a reasonable chance of fighting a disease, it can give false negatives that could lead to unnecessary booster vaccinations.

So where does this leave the average dog owner? My recommendation is to treat vaccine administration as a medical procedure

and as such, to consider the benefits as well as risks when deciding whether to use them. Talk to your veterinarian about your concerns. In return, listen to the reasoning he or she used in determining the frequency recommended for vaccination (which comes from practical experience). If you believe your veterinarian has your pet's best interest in mind, then the choice is usually very easy. Keep in mind, however, that sometimes, the frequency of vaccination (particularly for rabies) may be determined by local law.

Infectious Diseases and Vaccines

In the United States, vaccines are divided into two classes. "Core" vaccines are those that the American Veterinary Medical Association (AVMA) recommends for every dog, and "noncore" vaccines are limited to certain dogs, depending on their species and environment. The choice to use noncore vaccines depends on a number of variables, including age, breed, the health status of the dog, the potential for exposure, the type of vaccine, and how common the disease is to the geographical area where the dog lives. So, dogs that are not boarded probably do not need all the vaccinations against "kennel cough," and the Lyme disease vaccine should be administered only if you live in an area where it is prevalent. It is important to note that some core and noncore vaccines are given by veterinarians in what are called combination vaccines. These are single injections that will deliver the vaccines for as many as five different contagious diseases. Determining what "combination" and noncore vaccines as well as the type and frequency of booster immunizations your dog receives is a decision you will have to make with the advice of your veterinarian.

The four core vaccines will immunize your Shih Tzu against canine distemper, canine hepatitis, parvovirus, and rabies. Recently, however, a report from the AVMA recommends adding canine adenovirus-2 (presently classified as noncore) to the core vaccines. Noncore vaccines also exist for bordetellosis, parainfluenza, leptospirosis, coronavirus, and Lyme disease. Chances are that your breeder will have your puppy up to date on her immunizations when you get her, and your veterinarian can tell you when to schedule any additional vaccinations that are necessary.

Of Worms and Worming

Worms are by far the most common internal parasite found in dogs. There are four major types of worms that live in the digestive tract of the infected animal (roundworms, hookworms, whipworms, and tapeworms) and one major type that attacks the heart muscle (heartworms). The eggs of the digestive-tract worms, and sometimes adult worms themselves, can be found in the dog's stool. The eggs are microscopic, so if you suspect your dog has worms, you will have to take a stool sample to the veterinarian so the proper medication can be given.

Digestive-Tract Worms

To keep your Shih Tzu free of digestive-tract worms, your veterinarian should perform an annual stool check. Early detection and treatment will help prevent malnutrition, diarrhea, and stress-related immune suppression. It will also lessen the risk of transmission of these parasites from pet to pet, as well as from pets to people (especially children).

Symptoms of worm infestation include diarrhea, cramps, irregular appetite, weakness, poor coat condition, bloated belly, blood in the stool, and, in severe cases, paralysis. Depending on the identification of the type of worm detected, treatments may be in the form of an oral or injectable de-wormer.

Heartworm

Once found only along the south eastern seacoast, heartworm can now be found throughout the United States and is transmitted through mosquito bites. There are presently more than 60 species of mosquito known to transmit this illness. Heartworms spend their adult life attached to the right side of a dog's heart and the large blood vessels that attach the heart to the lungs. They can also be found in other species of animals but are rarely seen in humans.

Severely infected dogs can host several hundred adult heartworms, which can live for five to seven years. This puts a great strain on an infected dog's heart, which becomes enlarged, has to work harder, ages rapidly, and eventually weakens. Adult worms can obstruct the heart chambers and blood vessels between the heart and lungs. If a worm dies, it can block the flow of blood to smaller vessels, thus causing any number of circulation-related problems. Symptoms include coughing, decreased appetite, weight loss, and lethargy. In rare situations where infestations are very severe, the dog may die of sudden heart failure.

The best way to deal with heartworms is to use preventive medications, but it is important to understand that these do not kill the adult worms. In addition, if preventives are used when adult heartworms are present other severe problems can result. It is, therefore, very important to have your dog tested by your veterinarian for the presence of heartworms before starting any medications. If fully grown worms are present, they need to be treated with an adulticide or through surgical procedures.

There are a number of heartworm preventives available, and some will also help control other parasites. The two most popular are ivermectin and milbemycin. It is suggested that preventive medications be used year-round, even in areas where mosquitoes occur only-seasonally. If given continuously, the preventive will stop the worms from developing into adults. The choice of medications should be discussed with your veterinarian so you can learn the pros and cons of each.

External Parasites

At some point practically every dog will experience some form of discomfort caused by external parasites, such as fleas, ticks, or mites. These parasites can be extremely irritating to pets (as well as their owners) and cause serious skin problems. In addition, they can be the carriers of many diseases.

Fleas

The most common of canine parasites, fleas cause more pain and suffering than any other ailment. Fleas flourish when the weather turns warm and humid, so depending on the climate in which you live, fleas may be a seasonal or year-round problem. They differ from other parasites in that their strong hind legs enable them to jump long distances from one dog (or other warm-blooded host) to another. Adult fleas are dark brown and about the size of a sesame seed. They are highly mobile, and once they crawl under a dog's thick coat, they can move rapidly over the skin.

You may not know when your pet has a small infestation, but it is possible for ten adult fleas to produce well over 250,000 offspring in a month, so if left untreated, it will be only a matter of time before your Shih Tzu begins to show obvious signs of discomfort. Symptoms of flea infestation range from mild redness of the skin to severe scratching that can lead to open sores and skin infections. Another sign of flea infestation is the presence of small black flea "droppings" (about the size of finely ground black pepper) that the parasite leaves on your pet's coat. The excrement is dried blood meal, so if you put some of the powder on a damp white tissue, it will turn a rusty red-brown color as it dissolves. You may also see adult

fleas, along with the excrement, if you use a flea comb on the infested dog.

Fleas feed by biting their host and sucking their blood, so a Shih Tzu with heavy flea infestations can become anemic. Some dogs are allergic to flea saliva, which results in even more irritation and scratching. Where infestations are very heavy, fleas have been known to bite humans. With modern medicines, prevention of flea infestations is much easier and safer than it was in the past. There are several topical flea adulticides on the market today that are very effective preventives and last up to 30 days per dose. They do not require the

flea to ingest blood and can kill the flea before it bites or lays eggs.

Ticks

These dangerous bloodsucking parasites can be found in just about all countries worldwide. They are of particular concern because some of them carry and transmit disease.

Tick populations and the diseases associated with them vary demographically. The most common tick found in the United States is the "brown dog tick," which is large enough to be seen with the human eye. Although not all brown ticks are dangerous, it has been impli-

===== **TIP** =====

Tick Removal

You can remove ticks by carefully using tweezers to firmly grip the tick as close to the pet's skin as possible and gently pulling the tick free without twisting it. After removing the tick, you can crush it (while avoiding contact with fluids that can carry disease) or immerse it in a dilute solution of detergent or bleach.

If you live in an area where tick-borne diseases are known to occur, you can place the tick in a tightly sealed container and bring it to the veterinarian for examination. Do not attempt to smother the tick with alcohol or petroleum jelly, or apply a hot match to it, as this may cause the tick to regurgitate saliva into the wound and increase the risk of disease. Although humans cannot "catch" a tick-borne disease from an infected dog, they can become infected if they are bitten by a tick that is transmitting the disease.

cated as a carrier of Rocky Mountain spotted fever and babesiosis. These two diseases have similar symptoms, including fever, anorexia, depression, lethargy, and a rapid pulse rate. Another disease carrier is the deer tick, which is much smaller and barely perceptible to the human eye. It is this diminutive tick that is responsible for the spread of Lyme disease.

Dogs that frequent grassy and wooded areas populated by wild mammals have the great-est risk of exposure to ticks. Both the nymph and adult stages feed on animals. Unfed ticks resemble small crawling bugs, but once they attach themselves and begin to feed on their host, they begin to swell with blood until they look like a dried raisin. As they continue to gorge, they swell like a miniature balloon. Ticks are most often found around a dog's neck, in the ears, in the folds between the legs and body, and between the toes. Tick bites can cause skin irritation, and heavy infestations can cause anemia. If you take your Shih Tzu to tick-prone areas for fun or exercise, be sure to examine her for ticks immediately upon returning home and remove them from your pet. Prompt removal of ticks is very important, because it lessens the chance of disease transmission. Pets at risk for ticks can be treated using preventive flea adulticides. Your veterinarian can recommend the product best suited to your needs.

Lice

Like most external parasites, lice are bloodsuckers and their bite causes irritation. They will spend their entire lives among the hair of their hosts. When they lay their eggs (called nits), they become firmly attached to the victim's hair. If your dog is infested, you can see the egg clusters attached to the hairs. Lice can be very dangerous, so bring your dog to the veterinarian if you spot eggs. Lice can be readily treated with insecticidal products.

Mites

Mites are very small parasites that do their damage by burrowing into a dog's skin, causing intense itching. Mites are no bigger than a pinhead, and require a microscope for proper identification. When they burrow into the skin in large numbers, they can cause a serious skin disease called mange. Mange can occur in healthy dogs, but a clean, sanitary environment is the best deterrent. This condition is more typically found in dogs that frequent unsanitary places and suffer from improper nutrition. There are three principal forms of mites that infest dogs: ear mites, sarcoptic mange mites, and demodectic mange mites.

The symptoms of mite infestations are severe itching, and the crusting/scabbing of infected areas. Mange is usually treated using topically applied medications, but in many cases, cleaning and sanitizing the affected dog's environment is also necessary. Some forms of mange can be transmitted to humans. People who come into close contact with a carrier dog can develop skin rashes.

Common and Hereditary Ailments

Practically all purebred dogs have a predisposition for many diseases and ailments that are the result of poor breeding practices somewhere in their genealogy, or caused by their anatomical structure, and the Shih Tzu is no exception. It cannot be stressed enough that breeding practices (heredity), the environment, and socialization are all important factors that affect the health of an individual Shih Tzu. Responsible breeders spend their lifetime building a high-quality bloodline and certifying the health of their dogs. Some of the quality checks that Shih Tzu breeders attain for their dogs include OFA (Orthopedic Foundation for Animals) testing for hip and elbow dysplasia and patellar luxation, and CERF (Canine Eye

Registration Foundation) certification for hereditary eye ailments. Dogs shown to have any of the genetically linked ailments described here should not be used for breeding for fear of perpetuating the disease.

Eye Disorders

The Shih Tzu is prone to several genetically linked eye disorders. Although veterinarians may be very good at offering advice, you may have to see an eye specialist should your dog be diagnosed with one of these ailments.

Juvenile Cataracts

If left untreated, juvenile cataracts can lead to blindness. Cataracts form when the eye lens becomes cloudy or opaque, which cause the dog's vision to become blurred and eventually lost. Old-age cataracts can be found in almost every breed of dog, but they are not related to the juvenile form that can plague the young dogs of genetically involved breeds. Juvenile cataracts come in two forms: those that will dissolve and can be treated with cortisone eyedrops, and the non-dissolving type. Shih Tzu that have the nondissolving form will need to have an ophthalmologist determine if the retinas are normal before considering surgical removal of the cataract.

Distichiasis

A genetically linked eye disorder, distichiasis is caused by a dog's eyelashes growing incorrectly and coming into contact with the cornea. This is very irritating to the victim. Symptoms include squinting, excessive tearing, and inflammation. Electrolysis may be a temporary solution, but surgery is usually required to permanently correct the problem.

Entropion

Entropion is a hereditary condition in which the eyelid rolls inward so that the lashes rub on the cornea. Entropion can cause severe corneal damage, and can be treated only by surgical procedures, which for the majority of cases is fairly simple and effective. In more severe cases the surgery can be much more involved and even require multiple procedures to correct the alignment.

Progressive Retinal Atrophy (PRA)

A hereditary disease, PRA causes specialized dim-light receptors in the retina to slowly deteriorate, which will lead to night blindness. As the disease progresses, it leads to the deterioration of the bright-light receptors, resulting in complete blindness. There are no outward symptoms of this disease, but it is characterized by a Shih Tzu having trouble seeing in the dark. Because of the slow progression it is usually not seen until a dog is at least a year old. Unfortunately there is no treatment for PRA, nor is there any therapy for slowing its progress.

Lagophthalmos

Lagophthalmos means "rabbit eye" and is commonly seen in the Shih Tzu. This syndrome is a result of a combination of anatomical features including a protrusion of the eyeball, the inability to completely close the eyelids, and an exceptionally large eyelid opening. It can sometimes be detected in dogs whose eyelids do not cover the entire eye while they are asleep; however, a Shih Tzu may not exhibit any signs of this ailment for years, when it can result in increased pigmentation forming on the cornea and nose side of the eye. It

results in chronic irritation of the eye, and the increased exposure of the eyeball causes tears to evaporate at an increased rate. This ailment can commonly lead to a corneal ulcer developing in the middle of the eye. Lagophthalmos usually requires surgery to prevent further damage that can cause the eye to rupture.

Dry Eye (Keratoconjunctivitis Sicca)

The term *dry eye* refers to a change in the condition of the eye caused by a lack of tear production. There are many causes of dry eye including hypothyroidism, infections of the tear glands, nerve damage that affects the tear glands, or even the toxic effect of some sulfa-containing medications. Treatment for this ailment is primarily determined by the cause of the problem, but can include topical anti-inflammatory drugs, antibiotics, and artificial tear ointments or drops. Most Shih Tzu that have dry eye will do well if medications are administered quickly and regularly. For patients that do not do well on medications, surgery may be needed to move a duct from a saliva-producing gland to the eye. If left untreated, however, this ailment can lead to the loss of sight.

Skeletal Disorders

Hip Dysplasia

Hip dysplasia, an inherited developmental disorder of the hip joints, occurs most commonly in large breeds, but is also seen in the Shih Tzu. The condition is caused by a malformation of the hip socket that does not allow the proper fit of the head of the femur. At birth the hip of the affected dog appears nor-

mal, and signs of a problem may not appear until the dog is at least five to nine months of age. Hip dysplasia results in the painful inflammation of the hip joint, which leads to permanent physical damage, including lameness, and loss of the use of the back legs. Overfeeding, overexercising, and injury can also contribute to a young Shih Tzu damaging her hips.

Treatment for this ailment is to surgically correct the shape of the hip socket, or to perform a total hip replacement. Although these surgeries have a high success rate, they are performed only by a small number of specialists and can be quite costly. If you are planning to breed your dog, be sure to have her certified free of hereditary hip dysplasia by the OFA.

Elbow Dysplasia

Elbow dysplasia is normally associated with fast-growing puppies of large breeds, but is also seen in the Shih Tzu. It is not a simple condition to explain or understand, because elbow dysplasia is a syndrome of one or more other severe conditions, including arthritis and malformations of the elbow joint. It is not normally seen until a puppy is six to nine months old. Symptoms include obvious limping, holding the leg out from the body when walking, or trying to

walk without putting any weight on the front legs. In dogs with this condition, the symptoms become less severe as the dog matures; however, as the dog continues to mature, there will most likely be permanent arthritic changes to the joint. The patient can be made more comfortable with oral or injectable medications, and for some dogs, your veterinarian may recommend surgery. Although this surgery has been totally successful in eliminating the problem in some dogs, it may (depending on the severity) continue to be a lifelong problem for others.

Patellar Luxation

The patella (kneecap) is a small bone that guards the Shih Tzu's knee joint. This bone sits in a groove in the femur and is held in place by ligaments and muscles. Patellar luxation occurs when the bone can slide in and out of its proper position. It can be hereditary or can be caused by injury, poor alignment, weak ligaments, or a malformation of the femur. Symptoms include limping, a hopping gate while running, or carrying the leg off the ground. In severe cases surgery may be required. Weight control is also an important part of treating this disease, as excessive weight will cause undue stress on the joints, increasing the level of discomfort and pain.

Other Disorders

Constipation

As with humans, constipation in dogs is usually related to dietary issues. A lack of fiber or fresh water can disrupt a Shih Tzu's digestive system, and ingesting foreign objects, such as bones, rocks, or garbage, can also cause intestinal blockages. Constipation can also be caused by a lack of exercise, worm infestations, or medications that a dog may be taking.

The treatment used for constipation depends on the cause. If your dog is passing hard dry stools, then you can try adding fresh vegetables or ½ teaspoon of bran to each meal to see if the stool softens. Make sure there is always fresh water available to drink, and exercise your dog an hour after each meal. In chronic or severe cases, or when you know the cause is the ingestion of a foreign object, you should bring your dog to the veterinarian immediately.

Hot Spots and Moist Eczema

Also known as summer sores, hot spots can occur anywhere on the body and spread rapidly. Although hot spots can be caused by a variety of factors, the most common is bacterial infections, which can occur any time a dog's skin becomes irritated and broken. Whenever these infections are provided a warm, moist environment (from baths, wet grass, licking, and so on), they can easily spread. Hot spots do seem to be more prevalent in the summer, most likely because hot weather will promote bacterial growth. It can penetrate very deeply into the skin, causing severe itching, resulting in a dog that excessively scratches and licks in an attempt to gain some relief. This only adds to the spread of the disease.

Hot spots that are bacterial in nature can be treated with oral or topical antibiotics. Because the infection can penetrate deeply into the skin, keeping your Shih Tzu well groomed and free of matted hair (or perhaps even shaving the coat) will help to keep the problem in check. Providing your dog with a proper diet will help to keep her skin and coat in optimum condition and reduce the scratching that can lead to the development of this ailment.

Umbilical Hernias

These hereditary hernias are characterized by the presence of an abnormal opening in the dog's abdomen, which allows part of the abdominal contents to protrude through. This opening is usually the result of a birth defect. The problem can be surgically corrected once the Shih Tzu is six months of age. The procedure consists of stitching the opening closed. If the opening is small, your veterinarian may recommend putting off surgery to see if it closes on its own. If surgery is performed, the dog's activities will need to be restricted for a few weeks after the operation.

Juvenile Renal Dysplasia (JRD)

JRD is attributed to a developmental or genetic defect in the kidneys. The disease usually progresses in three stages. Stage one is the loss of nephrons over a period of months or years, with no symptoms being present. Stage two occurs after 70 percent of the nephrons are not functioning. Stage two symptoms include excessive thirst, greater volume of urine, weight loss, lethargy, and a loss of appetite. In the third stage vomiting, weakness, dehydration, and severe debilitation are added to second-stage symptoms, and death from renal failure is the eventual outcome. This disease has no cure, but through prescribed treatments the length and quality of the patient's life can be improved. These treatments include feeding the dog a low-protein/low-phosphorus diet to minimize the production of uremic toxins, administration of IV fluids to correct

disturbances caused by the toxins, and certain drugs that can help treat the anemia associated with chronic renal failure.

Von Willebrand's Disease

A common inherited disease, Von Willebrand's is a form of hemophilia: a bleeding disorder caused by defective blood platelet function that does not allow the blood to clot properly. In addition to excessive or continuous bleeding from injuries, symptoms of this disease include nosebleeds, bleeding from the gums, or blood in the urine or stool. All Shih Tzu should be tested for the presence of this disease, as it is extremely important that both you and your veterinarian know if your dog has a blood-clotting defect. If an afflicted dog becomes injured or requires surgery, the veterinarian will need to take special precautions. There is no cure for this disease, but several treatment options are available, depending on the severity of the disorder. Treatments range from providing blood-clotting medications (such as vitamin K) in oral or intranasal form, to extensive plasma transfusions.

Stenotic Nares

Stenotic nares is another congenital disorder found in Shih Tzu that is the result of the anatomical structure of their short muzzles. This defect is characterized by a malformation of the nostrils that causes them to have very narrow openings, thus restricting the puppy's ability to take in air. The main symptom of this defect is difficulty in breathing through the nostrils, and most puppies compensate by breathing through the mouth. Surgery to open the nares is usually very successful and will allow puppies to live relatively normal lives.

Cleft Palate

Cleft palate is a congenital defect that occurs when the bone and tissue on the roof of a puppy's mouth do not fuse together during development in the womb. This ailment can vary in size and can include the hard palate, the soft palate, or both. Puppies with this ailment usually have problems eating and are prone to developing pneumonia because food can end up in their airways and lungs. Symptoms include difficulty eating, noisy breathing, gagging, coughing, and thick mucous discharge. It is also believed that this ailment can be caused by excessive vitamin intake (or deficiencies) or corticosteroids prescribed to the pregnant mother. Occasionally a cleft palate may close on its own; otherwise the only option is surgery.

Shock

Shock is caused by lack of blood flow to meet the dog's needs, so any condition that adversely affects the heart or blood volume can induce shock. It can be brought on by hemorrhages, poisoning, and dehydration, but in dogs the most common cause is being hit by a car. The symptoms of shock, which are the result of inadequate blood circulation, are a drop in body temperature, shivering, listlessness, depression, weakness, cold feet and legs, and a weakened pulse.

If your dog is in shock, keep her calm and speak to her in a soft, reassuring voice. If the shock is caused by blood loss from an open wound, you will need to control the bleeding. Let your dog get into a comfortable position that causes the least amount of pain and makes breathing easier. Cover the dog with a blanket or a coat (but not too tightly) to keep her warm. Because the actions of a dog in shock can be unpredictable, you need to use caution when handling her. As they are small dogs, a sick or injured Shih Tzu can be carried, but a blanket "stretcher" can also be used to transport her. When possible, splint or support broken bones before moving your dog, and carry her with the injured parts protected. Use a muzzle only when absolutely necessary, as it can impair the dog's breathing, and bring her immediately to a veterinarian.

Broken Bones

Fractures and broken bones are also frequently the result of auto accidents. A dog with a fracture will be in severe pain, so approach her with caution, as she may attempt to bite. If the dog has a compound fracture (where the broken bone has punctured the skin), cover the wound with gauze or a clean cloth to prevent infection, and bring the injured dog to a veterinarian as soon as possible. Any fracture, simple or compound, requires professional attention.

Just as in humans, your veterinarian will use splints, casts, steel plates, and screws to realign the bone and allow it to heal. The treatment used will depend on the severity of the injury, the type of bone that is broken, and the age of the Shih Tzu. Growing puppies heal faster than geriatric dogs, so your veterinarian may decide to use a cast on a puppy but use pins for the same injury to an older dog.

Bleeding

To control bleeding you should immediately apply direct pressure to the source of the hemorrhage. Any absorbent material or piece of clothing can be used as a compress including

CHECKLIST

Items to Have in a First Aid Kit

- Elastic bandages
- Sterile nonstick dressing
- Antibiotic cream or ointment
- Scissors
- Cotton balls and swabs
- Antiseptic solutions
- Saline solution
- Digital thermometer
- Sterile ophthalmic ointment
- Tongue depressors
- Tourniquet
- Tweezers
- Alcohol
- Adhesive tape
- Snake bite kit (if you have poisonous snakes where you live)

gauze, towels, or shirts. Be sure to muzzle the dog before doing so.

Pressure should be applied for no less than five minutes. If bleeding continues after this time, secure the compress using gauze, a belt, pantyhose, or a necktie, and immediately seek the help of a veterinarian. If a leg is involved, then pressure applied to the upper portion of the limb will help to reduce the flow of blood. If a tourniquet is needed, it can be applied just above the wound, using a belt, necktie, or pantyhose. A pencil, ruler, or thin piece of wood can be used to twist and tighten the tourniquet until the bleeding has minimized. To prevent permanent damage to the leg, you should be able to pass one finger between

the tourniquet and the skin without too much effort. You should also release the pressure on the tourniquet for 30 seconds every 10 to 15 minutes.

Poisoning

Humans and dogs live their lives surrounded by poisons and toxins. Dogs, however, cannot read warning labels, which puts them at an extreme disadvantage. Most cases of dog poisoning are the result of ingestion, and more rarely through inhalation or absorption through the skin. Unfortunately, despite the best intentions of their owners, poisoning is common in dogs because of their curious nature and indiscriminating taste. The amount of damage a poison does is related to the amount the dog ingests (inhales, absorbs) and how long it has been in the body before treatment. If treatment is immediate, some poisons will not have any effect, whereas others, regardless of the speed at which the treatment is administered, can be fatal or result in permanent damage

The effect of a poison may not always be immediately seen. Some will not cause illness for a few days to a week or more, but most common poisons result in symptoms that can be seen within three to four days of exposure. Because of this time lapse, you should never wait if you see your Shih Tzu ingesting any potentially harmful substance. If you see your dog ingest anything she should not, read the label for warnings and the proper therapy or antidote you should use. You can call your veterinarian or poison control center (whose phone numbers you should always have on your telephone) for the recommended course of treatment. Taking immediate action can

Normal Physiologic Values for a Shih Tzu

Temperature	Pulse (beats per minute)	Respirations (per minute)
101.5–102.5°F (38.6–39.2°C)	90–120	18-24

sometimes mean the difference between life and death, so there may be times when you need to take action yourself. Be sure to report all toxic ingestions to your veterinarian as soon as possible.

Some of the most common poisons found in most people's homes are antifreeze, acetaminophen, pesticides, and lead-based paints. Fortunately, most of these have known antidotes, but not all poisons do. Because of this, be sure to keep all potentially harmful substances away from your pets, and be sure your Shih Tzu is not in the area whenever you are using them.

Home Care for the Older Shih Tzu

As your dog ages, she will experience a gradual decline in her physical and sometimes mental capabilities. Small breeds such as the Shih Tzu usually are considered geriatric when they are between 10 and 14 years old. Like

TIP

Giving Medication Directly

Over the course of your Shih Tzu's life, it is very likely that you will need to give her medication. To administer a pill, follow these steps: Get the pill out, hold it with your thumb and index finger, and call the dog with a happy voice. Place the dog's hind end against a wall so she cannot back away from you. Using your other hand, gently grasp the dog's muzzle from the top with your thumb on one side and your fingers on the other. Squeeze behind the upper canine teeth and tilt the head back to automatically open her mouth. Use one finger, on the hand holding the pill, to push down between the lower canine teeth, and place the pill as far back into the dog's mouth as possible, making sure to get it over the "hump" of the tongue. Close the dog's mouth and hold it closed, lower the head into a normal position, and gently rub or blow on the dog's nose to help stimulate her to swallow. When you are finished, be sure to give the patient plenty of praise and a treat if her diet allows, which will make it easier to do the next time. You can also ask your veterinarian to show you how it is done, because seeing a live demonstration is a great way to learn.

Liquid or oral syringe medications can be given in much the same way as a pill. Be sure to shake the medicine and have it measured in a syringe or eyedropper before you call the dog. Once the mouth is open, place the tip of the syringe or eyedropper into the pocket formed between the dog's cheek and back teeth, and slowly administer the medication, with slight pauses to allow the dog to swallow it.

humans, geriatric dogs require special care from their owners to help minimize the effects of the aging process and to make their golden years as comfortable as possible.

Make sure that your pet's living and sleeping space is clean, warm, and protected. You should provide soft bedding, and limit the changes to the dog's environment, including prolonged changes in temperatures that many geriatric dogs cannot adjust to well. Older dogs may also have a harder time seeing, so be careful about placing new or potentially dangerous objects in locations where your dog usually moves. You can also consider stomping your feet as you approach your lounging dog to warn her of your presence. Should your Shih Tzu experience stiffening joints or arthritis, you should avoid picking her up unnecessarily, and you may need to consider building ramps that will provide easier access to your home. You can also consult with your veterinarian about using nonsteroidal anti-inflammatory drugs, such as ibuprofen, for relief of arthritic pain.

Groom your Shih Tzu, be sure to brush her teeth regularly, and provide her with the exercise an aging dog still needs to stay in peak health. Grooming helps promote healthy skin and coat, and gives you the opportunity to perform a home health exam. Check the dog's teeth and mouth for any dental problems or foul odors. Feel the skin for lumps, and look for skin sores or discharges from the eyes and ears. Feel the Shih Tzu's limbs and abdomen for swelling or signs of pain.

Unless otherwise directed by your veterinarian, routine exercise is very important to the geriatric Shih Tzu. Walk your dog as often as possible. Even if the dog does not walk well, a short daily walk will help improve her circulation and stimulate the heart muscles, and the change in environment will provide some mental stimulation.

Be sure your older dog always has access to fresh, clean water. If your Shih Tzu is having trouble getting up, it may become necessary for you to bring the water dish to your pet. If your dog has trouble moving, be extra careful about exposing her to extreme weather, as she may have trouble getting out of the sun or finding a warm corner when the weather gets colder. In these cases you will need to either keep the dog inside or be sure adequate shelter is nearby. In addition, dogs that have trouble moving or problems with their eyesight should not be left in elevated locations, such as on a table, couch, or stair, where they could injure themselves trying to get down.

Be careful not to let the older, less active dog become overweight. Feed your aging Shih Tzu a good-quality diet that is appropriate for her aging and mental needs. Avoid giving too many treats, as these can lead to unnecessary weight gain. If your dog always had free access to food, you may need to switch to feeding her once or twice a day to better monitor her food intake. If your dog has dental problems, it may become necessary to soften her food by adding water to hard kibble. Be sure to discuss all instances of unexpected weight gain (or loss) with your veterinarian, who may recommend a specific diet.

As your dog becomes older, you will need to pay even more attention to the indicators of health. Symptoms such as irregular breathing, excessive panting, bouts of whining, and weakness in the rear legs are all signs that you need to discuss with your veterinarian. Providing a good home and proper veterinary care can definitely help your Shih Tzu live a longer, happier life.

When It Is Time to Say Good-bye

During the course of dog ownership there is no more difficult decision you may have to make than when your loving and loyal friend has become terminally ill and will soon die. Although modern veterinary medicine has many ways to extend the life of our pets, there comes a point where it will no longer serve a useful purpose. If your dog becomes terminally ill and is experiencing severe and constant pain, aggressive medical attention will not extend her life but instead will prolong the dying process. Euthanasia is the act by which a veterinarian painlessly induces death, ending the suffering of a terminally ill animal. When

the time comes, you must be ready to consider your pet's feelings as well as your own. This is never an easy choice, but it has been made in the past by millions of pet owners who also loved their pets.

There is no universal guideline that will help every pet owner through the euthanasia process, and the grief that follows is a different experience for everyone. The most loving and caring of dog owners may deal with it by becoming cold and callous, whereas strong, objective owners may completely fall apart. This is a personal experience, where you need to decide what is best for you and your pet.

Most pet owners experience a strong and lasting sense of grief and loss after the passing of their beloved pets. This is partly because there is no one available who can relate to the personal bond that forms between a dog and her master, and partly because many people feel that talking about it will make them the subject of ridicule. The bereavement of a loving pet owner can often be self-critical and may even bring up memories of other losses in one's personal life. This can lead to sadness, helplessness, and clinical depression. There is nothing wrong with feeling grief, and a loving, caring pet owner has no need to apologize for it. If you feel the need to talk to someone who understands, a number of support groups specialize in pet-loss counseling. Never feel ashamed or belittle yourself for the strong feelings you felt for your pet, and know that you are not alone. You can look for these support groups on the Internet, or ask your veterinarian for the telephone number of your local Veterinary Medical Association so you can be directed to the nearest pet-loss specialist.

UNDERSTANDING YOUR SHIH TZU

Shih Tzu are complex creatures and if we are to better understand them, we must take a close look at the process by which dogs evolved, became domesticated, and were selectively bred to create the pure breed we know today.

Instinctive Behavior

All dogs, regardless of breed, can trace their ancestry back to a form of wild dog or wolf. These creatures lived in a specially structured society. To live together in harmony, the members of each pack had to conform to certain behavioral rituals. These rituals included ranking order and the marking of territories.

Ranking order is a process by which the stronger and more experienced members of the pack are placed at the top of the social ladder, whereas the younger and weaker ones are subordinate. In the pack, all dogs (with the exception of one) submit to the authority of higher-ranked dogs. This system prevents violent fights from breaking out, and helps the pack to hunt and coexist as a group, thereby ensuring the survival of the species. This behavior pattern is instinctive and can be

seen in all modern dogs. This behavior is what allows humans to train dogs. During the training process, you, the master, are enforcing your rank (or dominance) over your pet. If the dog did not accept her subordinate role, she would not follow your commands and instead attempt to force her dominance over you.

Scent marking is another instinctive behavior that the modern Shih Tzu has carried over from its wild ancestors. Although this trait is more important to males, it plays a role in every dog's life. As you walk your Shih Tzu, she will attempt to mark several spots, to let all the other dogs in the territory know she lives nearby. Female dogs in heat will also excrete a strong scent to attract mates. A male Shih Tzu will try to mark every prominent spot with his urine, including trees, fence posts, and telephone poles, to designate his territory. Likewise

all dogs will use their nose to interpret other scent marks to determine if they were made by friends or foes.

After the passing of countless generations of these wild dogs, these behavioral patterns eventually became instinctive. It is because dogs possess these instinctive behaviors that man was first able to domesticate them.

Effects of Domestication

Evidence indicates that dogs were first domesticated about 12,000 years ago. Undoubtedly, they were the first of all animals to be tamed by humans. It is believed that humans trained wolves, or wild dogs, to assist them in hunting. The hunting practices of both dogs and humans at this time were probably very similar. This made training them all the more simple.

During the course of domestication, dogs lost many of the behavioral rituals associated with pack life, but retained others. They also began to display new behavior patterns that they learned from their human trainers. Which traits were gained and which were lost depended greatly on the history of each particular breed and its relationship with humans.

Much of the Shih Tzu's history revolved around its association with the imperial family in the forbidden city of Peking. This close relationship with royalty is no doubt responsible for the proud and arrogant manner in which the Shih Tzu moves and behaves. These regal house pets were cherished and pampered by the royal family and their servants for hundreds of years. As a result of countless generations of pampering, the Shih Tzu has also developed a friendly disposition toward all people, a trait not found in all breeds of dogs.

Most of the physical attributes of the Shih Tzu are a result of the careful and select breeding practices used by the eunuchs of the royal court. These breeders would mate dogs based on their temperament as well as their physical qualities. The last thing the royal breeders wanted was to have their prized pooches snap at the emperor.

The nature of the Shih Tzu is, therefore, a blend of two elements. First is the instinctive behavior that has been retained from its wild ancestors. This behavior includes the sexual drive, the marking of territory, and submitting to a ranking order. Second are the traits for which the dog has been selectively bred, such as people-oriented behavior, which is the result of their being bred to become the perfect house pet of the Imperial Courts.

Communication

Dogs are not blessed with the ability to speak an intelligible language, so they must find other ways of communicating their thoughts and emotions to both humans and other dogs. All dogs will use body language, facial expression, and vocal sounds to convey their feelings. In order to understand your dog's moods, you should pay special attention to these signals.

Dogs do not make sounds simply to hear the sound of their own voices. Each noise they

===== **T I P** =====

When to Be Wary

Be wary of any dog that has her ears back, her upper lips raised and mouth open, and the hair on the back of her neck raised. These are all warning signs of fear and/or anger, and they may precede an attack.

make is for a reason. Every sound reflects a mood. A dog will whimper and whine when she is lonely; yelp in fright; howl in pain; groan in contentment; bark in anger, alarm, or glee; and make a variety of sounds when she is seeking attention.

The bark of the Shih Tzu is unique. Unlike other toy breeds, the Shih Tzu does not exhibit noisy yapping. Instead, she will give one short, sharp bark, which fades into a series of throaty groans. The Shih Tzu will use this sound to express a variety of moods. Often you must look for additional signs to determine the purpose of the sound.

Body language is another good indicator of your dog's mood. A happy dog may jump up and down and bark. A dog that crouches and lowers her head to the floor may be showing signs of fear. Many times you can get insight into your dog's emotions by examining her tail. A briskly wagging tail is a sign of joy. The happier the dog is, the more her tail will wag. A frightened dog will lower her tail, and perhaps put it between her legs.

As a final indicator of your dog's mood, examine her ears and muzzle. A contented Shih

Dog/Human Age Equivalents

Dog's Age	Human's Age	Dog's Age	Human's Age
2 months	14 months	7 years	49 years
3 months	3 years	8 years	56 years
6 months	6 years	9 years	63 years
8 months	10 years	10 years	65 years
12 months	17 years	11 years	71 years
18 months	21 years	12 years	75 years
2 years	25 years	13 years	80 years
3 years	30 years	14 years	84 years
4 years	36 years	15 years	87 years
5 years	40 years	16 years	89 years
6 years	42 years	17 years	95 years

Tzu will have a closed mouth and normally set ears. An alert or attentive dog will raise her ears. Sometimes she will cock her head inquisitively to one side. Should you encounter a dog whose ears are back and upper lips raised, exposing the teeth, be very cautious. These are signs of a very frightened or angry dog. Many times these signals precede an attack.

The Sense Organs

Most dogs do not have a very good sense of sight. Instead they rely more on their senses of smell, hearing, taste, and touch. Because of its long history as a house dog, the Shih Tzu also lacks much of the ability to discriminate between scents, a sense that is exceptional in some of the larger breeds. The sense of smell is very important to some dogs, such as the hunting or herding dogs. It is, however, of little practical use to a lap dog. Much of the Shih Tzu's ability to discriminate between

different scents has simply disappeared because of a lack of use.

What the Shih Tzu lacks in her ability to smell is more than made up for in her ability to hear. The Shih Tzu possesses a highly developed sense of hearing, which is significantly superior to that of a human. They can hear a wider range of sounds, especially those in the high-pitched frequencies. Shih Tzu have no trouble hearing the silent call of the Galton whistle. They can also hear sounds from a much greater distance than a human.

The Shih Tzu does not have the ability to focus her eyes sharply on an object, but her peripheral vision is much greater than that of a human. Because of this, the Shih Tzu's eyes are much more sensitive to motion. They must, however, rely more on their sense of hearing to interpret what they see.

The long coat of the Shih Tzu does not take away greatly from its sense of feeling. These tiny dogs are much more sensitive to touch

than many other long-haired breeds. The Shih Tzu's sense of feeling, however, is not as great as that of a human.

It is believed that the Shih Tzu, like all other dogs, may possess other senses that we do not completely understand. One of these is a dog's innate sense of navigation. We have all heard reports of dogs traveling hundreds of miles to find their home, yet we do not fully comprehend how it is done.

Life Changes

In her first weeks in your home, your puppy is extremely impressionable. It is during this time that she begins to learn the rules of the house and starts to form her relationship with her owner. During this time, you will use training as a method of curbing and satisfying your puppy's ever-growing curiosity.

As the puppy continues to grow, she will become more and more aware of her own physical attributes. With the passing of time, your puppy will begin to build up strength and improve her motor skills. Accompanying your dog's improvement in muscle conditioning is an increasing confidence in herself.

By the time your Shih Tzu is 12 or 13 weeks old, she will have become completely aware of herself and her environment. One of her favorite pastimes will be to share all of her discoveries with you. She will begin to investigate everything. During this stage, your puppy is still extremely impressionable, so treat her with care and continue to reinforce the rules of your house. This will be extremely important because of what lies ahead.

At seven to ten months old, your Shih Tzu will almost have reached full size. This is when the dog reaches sexual maturity, a period in time that is the equivalent of human adolescence. No longer will your puppy act with innocent curiosity. Instead, her actions will be bolder and more assertive. Just as a human teenager might do, your Shih Tzu will begin to test the system. This is when you will start to see just how effective all of your previous training methods have been.

Your Shih Tzu is now feeling extremely comfortable and confident with your lifestyle, and will naturally want to be included in all of your activities. While you have continued to train your puppy, and she should therefore know what is expected of her, there is a growing feeling in your dog that tells her otherwise. It is at this point that your Shih Tzu's instincts tell her that it is time to challenge you in order to improve her rank. Remember, this is all part of the natural ways of canine behavior. When it does occur, do not lose your temper. You must calmly, yet firmly, show your Shih Tzu that you are the authority. This will help lead your dog through her final stage of development.

Once your Shih Tzu reaches full maturity, she should not undergo any behavioral changes (with the exception of mating urges) until a ripe old age. Changes that occur during the geriatric years are more dependent on the individual dog and her medical background. With many aged dogs, changes in their routines or behavior are often the result of a medical problem brought on by old age. As the dog ages, she may undergo a deterioration of the digestive and immune systems, as well as a deteriorating skeletal-muscle condition.

The older dog may become lethargic or moody, lose her orientation, or experience hearing loss. She may even forget many learned responses. This may all sound dreadful, yet it is all part of the aging process. There is very little you can do to change the situation, except offer your devoted, loving pet your sympathy and understanding.

BASIC AND ADVANCED TRAINING

In all honesty, the Shih Tzu may not be as easy to train as some other breeds. However, they are very intelligent dogs, and there is no reason why they cannot learn any lesson you wish to teach them.

This chapter will describe some basic rules you must follow, and certain techniques you can use when teaching your Shih Tzu the basic commands and some advanced tricks. This chapter does not cover all of the skills a Shih Tzu can learn, but the same rules and techniques can be implemented to teach your dog an endless number of skills. How much and how well your Shih Tzu learns will be totally dependent upon your abilities as a trainer.

Why Dogs Learn

Your Shih Tzu has a history of instinctive behavior that goes back into time before they were first domesticated. These wild dogs were pack animals, and as such had to learn to function as a group in order to survive. Their coexistence was dependent upon the establishment of a ranking order that prevented serious fights within the pack. Ranking order is based primarily on strength and experience. In this system, smaller and weaker dogs have to submit to dogs of higher authority. Ranking order is an instinctive behavior that is still exhibited in our modern-day domesticated breeds.

During the training process, you will be showing your Shih Tzu that you and other members of your family are the authority to which she must submit. Once your puppy recognizes you as the pack leader, you can teach her the rules of your house.

Training a Puppy

The first lesson, teaching your puppy her name, will begin as soon as you bring the puppy home from the breeder. This will probably be the easiest of all lessons for your dog to understand. Every time you call your puppy,

CHECKLIST

The 10 Commandments of Training

In developing your training methods, there are certain do's and don'ts that must be followed. Adhere to these rules during training sessions.

1. **Thou shall maintain a positive atmosphere.** Hold each training session in an atmosphere conducive to learning, with as few distractions as possible. Never attempt to teach your puppy anything when you are in a bad mood.

2. **Thou shall be authoritative.** Your dog will understand tones better than words, and you must deliver all visual and verbal commands clearly and unmistakably. Reprimands must be sharp and firm, whereas praise must be calm and friendly. Never demonstrate your authority by using physical force.

3. **Thou shall be consistent.** All household members must decide what is permitted behavior and what is not. Once your dog has learned a lesson, never let her do the contrary without a reprimand.

4. **Thou shall teach only one new lesson per session.** Do not attempt to teach your puppy more than one new lesson in a single session, and never move on to a new concept until the dog has mastered the previous one. Once a lesson has been mastered, it can be included as a warm-up exercise in your dog's training regimen.

5. **Thou shall give credit where credit is due.** Praise your dog when she performs a command properly. Verbal praise, petting, a small treat, and/or scratching behind the ears will make your Shih Tzu an eager student.

6. **Thou shall schedule training sessions just before mealtime.** Toy dogs respond very well to "treat" rewards for successful execution of a command. Treats can keep a Shih Tzu's focus and attention on the trainer's hand.

7. **Thou shall punish disobedience immediately.** Because a puppy has a very short memory, you must never put off a reprimand. If, for example, your puppy chews a slipper, do not punish her unless you catch her in the act; otherwise she will not understand why you are displeased.

8. **Thou shall not hit.** Limit yourself to verbal reprimands; never hit or use physical force on your dog.

9. **Thou shall not bore your students.** Even when your dog is older, keep your training sessions short and end them early if the dog begins to lose interest. Likewise, never hold a training session when your dog is tired.

10. **Thou shall not delay training.** Begin working with your puppy the day you bring her home. Hold two or three sessions each day and hold them for as long as the puppy shows interest. In 10 to 15 minutes, you can provide sufficient teaching without boring the dog.

or give her commands, address her by her given name. Try not to call your Shih Tzu by any nicknames. This will only confuse her, and she may not respond when called.

Another early lesson your Shih Tzu will have to learn is the meaning of the word *"No."* It is inevitable that you will have to use this word several times on the first day alone. A mischievous puppy will always do something wrong during her explorations of your home. When this happens, tell her *"No"* in a sharp, firm tone that shows your puppy you are serious. Do not allow the puppy to misinterpret your warnings.

If the puppy refuses to listen, place her in her crate. *Never* hit your puppy, either with your hand or with a rolled-up newspaper. This will make your puppy fearful of you and hand-

shy of anyone who comes near her. Using a crate will simplify training and speed up the housetraining process.

Using Treats as a Training Aid

Using treats as a training aid can be very effective during the early learning phases. While some dogs respond very well to no more than a loving pat on the head for good behavior, others need a little more incentive to get them to respond consistently and appropriately. While treats can be that extra incentive, they need to be used correctly, so that they do not become dependent on them to demonstrate "good" behavior.

To this end, I recommend limiting the offering of treats to the early learning phases of

training. As an example, when teaching the *down* command, place the treat by your dog's nose and slowly lower it to the floor while you give the verbal command. When she lies down, give her the treat as a reward. Repeat until you are confident that the lesson is understood.

As you continue on with the training, replace the treat with verbal praise and patting. The goal is to have her respond to your verbal commands and hand signals in order to receive your praise. You can occasionally give a treat during the later training stages, but do not let her see it until you have a proper response to the command.

The only time I recommend consistently using treats is for the *come* command. This command can sometimes be difficult to teach

and you may need that extra incentive to have your Shih Tzu choose to come to you for a treat and verbal praise, rather than succumbing to the many other temptations that dogs seem to find on a regular basis.

In the upcoming sections, I refer to giving praise to the student whenever she successfully follows your command. Depending on the stage she is in, you will need to make the determination if that praise should be in the form of a treat reward, or verbal praise with patting.

Walking on a Leash

Because you will be taking your Shih Tzu for her scheduled outdoor elimination sessions, you must teach her how to walk on a leash. Begin this training from the first time you walk the puppy. Place a collar on the puppy, making sure that it is neither too tight nor too loose. Attach the leash, and begin your walk. Hold the leash on your right side and use gentle tugs or pulls to keep the puppy close to your leg. Do not allow the puppy to get under your feet. Also, do not let the puppy run ahead of you. If she tries to run ahead, restrain the puppy by using friendly persuasion with the leash. For the most part, though, your puppy will tend to fall behind because her legs are short and she is not capable of great speed. If your puppy should trail behind, remain patient. Use encouraging words and some gentle nudging to keep the puppy in the proper walking position.

Being Alone

A puppy must learn at an early age that she will be left alone on occasion. You must teach her how to behave when she is on her own, because a poorly trained puppy can cause a great deal of damage.

To accustom your puppy to being alone, leave her in a familiar room while you quietly go into an adjacent room where the puppy can neither see nor hear you. Stay there for five or ten minutes and then return. If the puppy has gotten into any trouble, reprimand her. Gradually increase the time the puppy is left alone in the room, reprimanding her when necessary, until she begins to act properly.

If you must leave before your puppy has gained your full trust, then place her in her crate with some food, water, and toys until you return. If you do not have a crate, lock the puppy in a familiar puppy-proof room with the same supplies and her sleeping box. Remove all tempting objects such as shoes, papers, and clothing.

No Begging Allowed

It never fails to amaze me just how many people intentionally (or unintentionally) teach their dogs to beg. Some people even think that seeing a dog beg is a cute or innocent act. Begging, however, is neither cute nor innocent. It is a very bad habit that should not be tolerated. A well-fed and properly trained dog should never have to beg.

Begging may start out very innocently. You are about to sit down to eat your big, juicy steak when you notice your beloved Fifi standing in the doorway staring at you (and your steak) with watery, pleading eyes. You must resist the temptation! Most people succumb, making a big mistake. They will call their beloved Shih Tzu to the table and reward her with a table scrap. You would not believe how this simple act of charity on your part can turn into such a nasty habit. Although you may not mind having Fifi as a constant table com-panion, think about how it may bother dinner guests in your home.

Begging must be stopped before it develops into a bad habit. If your Shih Tzu attempts to beg for table scraps, reprimand her with a scolding of *"No!"* Then point away from the table and toward the puppy's crate or sleeping box. After a short while, your puppy will learn to avoid the table during mealtimes.

Simple Commands

The simple commands that every puppy must learn are *sit, stay, come, heel,* and *lie down.* You should begin to teach your Shih Tzu these lessons when she is six months old. Hold your training sessions in a confined area so as to avoid distractions. Try to keep the sessions short (10 to 15 minutes) and limit them to two or three times a day, so you will not wear your puppy out. A tired puppy will be more resistant to learning. Another good tip is to train your puppy before she has eaten. A puppy may become sluggish and disinter-ested after a big meal. It is also wise to take your puppy for a walk and allow her to eliminate before each session. Learning her lessons will be hard enough without additional pressures.

When teaching your Shih Tzu the simple commands, use one- or two-word phrases when giving orders rather than long sentences. For example, say *"Sit, Fifi"* rather than *"Sit down next to me, Fifi."* Besides keeping the commands short, you must also use the proper tone of voice and gestures. Commands should be clear, firm, and sharp. If you accompany the verbal orders with an easily understood hand gesture, you can eliminate much of the confu-sion that a puppy might be experiencing.

Sit: The *sit* command can be taught just as easily indoors as outdoors. Fit your puppy with her leash and collar, and take her to an isolated room or a quiet area in your yard. Hold the leash about halfway down in your right hand, and place your left hand on the puppy's hindquarters. Then give the firm, sharp command of *"Sit!"* or *"Sit, Fifi,"* while pressing gently and steadily on her hindquarters. If your puppy begins to lower her head, gently pull the leash upward to prevent her from lying down. Once your puppy is seated, hold her down for a while and do not allow her to jump back up. Be sure to praise your dog thoroughly, and reward her with a small treat.

Repeat this procedure for the entire session or until the puppy begins to lose interest. Each time the command is performed, praise your dog's efforts. As your puppy begins to sit without any pressure being applied to her hindquarters, you can start to accompany the

verbal command with a hand gesture, such as a finger pointed toward the ground.

Do not expect your Shih Tzu to master this lesson in her first training session. If you repeat the procedure every day, your puppy will soon learn to sit. Once you feel confident of your Shih Tzu's abilities, remove the leash and give the command. If your dog has been trained properly, she should perform correctly. If not, remain patient, and repeat the procedure using the leash.

Stay: The *stay* command is usually a more difficult command to learn, especially for a devoted puppy that always wants to be by her owner's side. The *stay* command is very important because, on occasion, a dog's life may depend on obeying it. This command means that the dog should stand stationary wherever she is, and has been used to prevent many dogs from running in front of moving automobiles.

Once again, fit your puppy with her collar and leash. When teaching your puppy to stay, refrain from using her name with the command. On hearing her name, the dog may think that some action is expected from her. Begin this lesson by running through the *sit* procedure. Once the dog is seated, follow this with the command *"Stay!"* As you say this new command, raise your hand, palm toward the dog, like a police officer stopping traffic. Normally your dog will just cock her head and give you a bewildered stare. If the puppy should begin to stand up, however, reproach her with a sharp *"No!"*

Take up all the slack in the leash and hold your Shih Tzu in place. Repeat the procedure until your dog appears to understand. Then remove the leash and repeat the command several times. Each time the dog obeys,

praise her. Should she disobey, scold her with a sharp *"No!"*

Continue this procedure until your puppy has repeated it with regular success. Then slowly back away from the dog. As you walk backward, be sure to maintain eye contact with your student, and keep repeating the verbal command *"Stay!"* with your palm raised. Should your Shih Tzu begin to follow, give her a sharp *"Stay!"* If she continues, reprimand her. Naturally, you should give your beloved puppy great praise and a treat when she obeys.

Come: If you call out your puppy's name, she will probably race across the room to greet you. The real trick to the *come* command, however, is to have your puppy run to you when something of greater interest is attracting her

attention. Your job will be to train your Shih Tzu to come to your side whether she wants to or not.

Teach your Shih Tzu to come right after she has learned to sit and stay. Begin your session by running through the *sit* and *stay* procedures. Once she has stayed at a good distance, call the dog by name followed with the command *"Come."* Accompany the words with a lively sound or gesture such as clapping your hands or bending down and slapping your thighs. This will help excite your dog into motion.

Under most circumstances, your Shih Tzu will quickly learn this lesson, and you should praise each success. If the puppy remains stubborn and does not respond correctly, put her on a long rope and let her wander away. Then repeat the command *"Come,"* and begin to reel the rope in. Continue to repeat the command as the dog is drawn closer. When your puppy reaches your side, shower her with praise. Repeat this lesson several times, and then try it again without the rope.

Obedience Training

Two of the simple commands—*heel* and *down*—are considered part of a dog's obedience training because they are mandatory exercises for every dog that enters an Obedience trial. Even if you do not plan to enter your Shih Tzu in an Obedience trial, there are many obedience exercises that all dogs should learn. These skills will help you to handle your dog properly in awkward situations, and will reinforce your dog's understanding of the master/subordinate relationship.

Obedience Schools

Do not be misled: Obedience schools are not just for the problem or stubborn dog. These schools can teach both you and your dog all there is to know about competing in shows. Even if you are not planning to enter your Shih Tzu in an Obedience trial, these schools can offer an enjoyable and interesting alternative to training your dog alone. They provide a learning atmosphere and are run by experienced dog handlers who can supply you with expert advice and helpful training tips.

If there is an older child in your family, you can have him or her take your Shih Tzu to classes. This will help teach your child the

responsibilities of dog care. Working with a dog at obedience school will teach your child greater self-respect and also respect for the dog.

You can get the name of a reputable obedience school in your area from your Shih Tzu Club or the AKC. Before enrolling, be sure that the class is affordable and suits your purposes. Most schools offer separate classes for owners interested in showing, and others for amateurs.

Heel

When your Shih Tzu learns to heel properly, she will walk on your left side with her head about as far forward as your knees. Heeling prevents your dog from running across your feet and entangling you in the leash, or moving away and bumping into people. Although you will require a leash when you begin to teach this lesson, eventually your Shih Tzu must learn to heel without the restraint of a leash.

Begin by running through all the other commands your dog has mastered. This will help bolster the dog's confidence before you start this difficult lesson. Hold the end of the leash in your right hand, and stand with the dog by your left leg. Then remove all slack from the leash by grabbing the leash about halfway toward the collar with your left hand. Begin to walk briskly (by your Shih Tzu's standards), giving the sharp command *"Heel!"* or *"Heel, Fifi!"* Control and guide the dog's movements using your left hand. Do not allow the dog to run ahead, drop back, or stray from side to side. You must remain patient. Your dog may act unpredictably when faced with this new command.

As the lessons progress, remember to praise your dog for responding correctly, and reprimand her immediately for improper actions. Should your Shih Tzu continue to lag behind,

pull steadily on the leash to bring the dog even with your leg. Do not force your dog forward or drag her behind you. This will destroy your dog's confidence. If she lunges forward, pull her back to your side while repeating the *"Heel"* command. If you continue to have difficulty, run through the *sit, stay,* and *come* exercises before trying the *"Heel"* command again.

The *heel* lesson is very difficult for a dog to learn, so remain patient and try not to teach the lesson too quickly. Take your time and be sure your dog understands it thoroughly. Once your Shih Tzu has mastered the *heel* on a leash, take her through a turning exercise. If she has trouble heeling whenever you turn, take a shorter grip on the leash, and bring the dog closer to your side. Repeat the exercise, speaking a sharp-toned *"Heel!"* while using gentle persuasive force to keep the dog by your side. As your Shih Tzu's performance improves, take her through a series of straight-line, right-turn, and left-turn exercises. Once she has mastered turning, it is time to begin training on a slack leash.

Perform the heeling procedure with the leash, but do not exert any pressure on the dog's collar. At the dog's first mistake, grasp the leash firmly and lead the dog steadily in the proper direction. Praise her lavishly for her success.

When the dog has learned to walk correctly with a slack leash, it is time to try it without a leash. If your Shih Tzu has performed properly with a loose leash, there is no reason why she should not achieve the same results without it. Do not allow the dog to regress into any bad habits. Whenever she makes a mistake, your Shih Tzu should be given a verbal reprimand. If you continue to have trouble, repeat the *heel* lesson using the leash. It is important to do the exact same routine with and without the leash. If you do this and remember to praise a job well done, your Shih Tzu should learn to heel properly.

Down

By this point you should have no trouble having your dog assume the sitting position. Grab both of her front legs and pull them forward while saying *"Down."* If your dog attempts to stand up, give her a sharp *"No!"* If pulling on the front legs does not work, try pulling the legs forward while pushing down on the dog's shoulders, using steady pressure. While you are doing this, give the command *"Down!"* Since both of your hands will be occupied, you can carefully step on the leash to prevent the dog from returning to her feet. Keep the dog in the *down* position for about one minute.

As your Shih Tzu progresses, gradually increase the amount of time she must stay down. Once your dog has mastered this exercise, you must begin to move away. As with the *stay* command, move slowly backward while maintaining constant eye contact with your student. If you see the dog begin to stand, repeat the command *"Down!"* using the appropriate tone of voice. Repeat this until your Shih Tzu performs perfectly, making sure to praise her for her good efforts.

Relinquishing an Object

Teaching your dog to give up an object obediently will strengthen your master/subordinate relationship. It is a lesson that every good dog must understand.

Give your Shih Tzu a suitably sized piece of nonsplintering wood to play with and grasp with its teeth. Command the dog to sit, and praise her when her obeys. Then, using both hands, gently pry the dog's jaws apart, while saying *"Let go!"* in a strict and firm tone of voice. If the dog begins to growl, give her a sharp *"No!"* Do not be afraid if your Shih Tzu growls. This is only her way of trying to get you to back down, and thereby establish her dominance over you. Dogs will also growl at anyone or anything that attempts to steal their prey—in this case, the stick. It is important that you make your Shih Tzu know just who is the boss. You must take the object away and establish your mastery. Once the dog accepts you as a dominant force, she will give up the stick without objection.

Keep repeating this lesson until your dog will let go of the stick without you having to use any physical force. Remember to praise her whenever she performs well, and reprimand her for noncompliance. If your Shih Tzu proves to be extremely stubborn, you can confine her to her crate, should all else fail. Upon releasing the dog from the crate, you can try the lesson again.

Retrieving

Retrieving is not an act that will come naturally to any member of the toy-breed group. However, with time, patience, and perseverance, you will be able to teach your Shih Tzu this exercise. In addition to its importance as an obedience skill, retrieving can become a good way for you and your Shih Tzu to play together. The act of retrieving usually demands a lot more energy than the previously mentioned training lessons. So be sure to watch your dog closely, and stop your session as soon as the dog begins to tire.

Start by selecting a suitably sized nonsplintering stick, and have your dog sit next to you, facing forward. Throw the stick forward and call out the command *"Fetch!"* Provided that you did not throw the stick clear out of sight, your Shih Tzu will probably get up and begin to move toward it.

If your Shih Tzu picks up the stick in her mouth and returns to you, command the dog to sit, put your hand (palm up) under her lower jaw and say *"Let go!"* This, however, is not a very likely event. Teaching a Shih Tzu to retrieve is rarely this simple.

If your Shih Tzu shows no desire to return with the stick, repeat the exercise using a thin 30-foot (9-m) rope. Tie the cord to the dog's collar, throw the stick, and again call out *"Fetch!"* Once she has picked up the object, draw the dog toward you, then take the object from the dog while saying *"Let go!"*

You should be able to remove the object from the dog's mouth without any resistance. If the dog drops the stick, or refuses to pick it up in the first place, put it in the dog's mouth and then remove it, giving the relinquishing command. Keep repeating this lesson until the dog understands that the object is to be taken from her mouth.

When you begin the retrieving exercises, you should naturally start by throwing the stick only a short distance. As your confidence in your dog's ability grows, you can gradually increase the length of your throws.

Jumping over Hurdles

Like retrieving, jumping over hurdles is an unusual act for a Shih Tzu. However, it can be learned and later act as a form of play. Start by commanding your dog to sit on one side of a small pile of boards (about 3 inches [7.5 cm] high) while you stand on the opposite side. Command your dog by saying *"Jump!"* If the dog walks around the boards, give her a verbal reprimand, then bring her back and start over. Praise your dog for a successful performance.

Once your Shih Tzu learns to leap over the hurdles on command, you can gradually increase the height of the obstacle. Be careful not to make the boards too high, for an accident could hurt a young dog, and will discourage further jumping.

Once the dog learns to jump the obstacle on command, begin a jump-and-retrieve exercise. Place the stick to be retrieved on the far side of the hurdle. Command the dog to sit by your side. Then command her to retrieve the stick by saying *"Jump! Fetch!"* Make sure that these commands are given in a clear, firm voice. The dog, upon hearing these commands, should leap over the hurdle, pick up the stick, and return over the boards. Tell the dog to sit again, and take the stick from her mouth, saying *"Let go!"* Naturally, such a great effort demands from you the greatest praise.

Training Problems

If, during the course of your training sessions, you should meet a roadblock, remain patient and understanding. Never force your Shih Tzu to learn. Try to keep your sessions enjoyable for both you and your devoted companion. Anger and extreme physical force have never helped a dog learn anything. In fact, they only serve to destroy a learning atmosphere, and will cause your Shih Tzu to lose her confidence and trust in you.

In most cases, you will find that your teaching caused the problem. If, after reevaluating your methods, you feel that this is not the problem, then examine your Shih Tzu and her environment. Perhaps your Shih Tzu is being distracted by an outside factor. If so, then remove the cause before proceeding. If you suspect an illness, make an appointment to see your veterinarian.

If you continue to encounter difficulties, I strongly urge you to contact a reputable obedience school.

Remember to begin training your Shih Tzu while she is still young. However, never force her to learn too much in too short a time. Take your time and make sure the dog understands each lesson thoroughly before proceeding to the next. If you do everything in a correct and timely fashion, there are really few limits to what your Shih Tzu can learn. Unfortunately, it will not be until the dog grows into a mature, well-behaved adult that you begin to reap the fruits of your training labors. Keep in mind, however, that every ounce of energy you put into training will be given back tenfold. In later years, you and your Shih Tzu will be able to enjoy innumerable hours of wonderful companionship.

The Shih Tzu in Competition

Many Shih Tzu owners are attracted to participating in dog shows because it combines the excitement of competition with a chance to spend more quality time with their dogs. In the United States the American Kennel Club (AKC) sponsors many events, attracting millions of participants. These events include conformation shows, obedience trials, field trials, hunting tests, agility trials, Canine Good Citizen tests, lure coursing, herding trials, and tracking tests. Although Shih Tzu are technically able to compete in many of these events, it's most common to find them competing in conformance shows and Good Citizen tests.

Should you decide to try the show ring, keep in mind that no individual dog can please everyone. It would be great if your Shih Tzu delighted each judge she met, but you should not count on this happening—dogs of that caliber are extremely rare. It is much more important that your dog please you. Never blame your dog for failure in the ring. If it were up to your Shih Tzu, she would win every award possible to please you. So go to the shows, have a good time, and learn all you can. Afterward, bring your beloved companion back home and show her that you still believe that she is the best dog in the world.

Conformation Events

Conformation events are shows in which the quality of the breeding stock is evaluated (meaning spayed or neutered dogs cannot compete in them). In these shows, a Shih Tzu is judged on her appearance, physique, bearing, temperament, and how well the dog conforms to the breed standard.

There are three types of conformation dog shows: all-breed shows, specialty shows for a specific breed, and group shows, which are limited to dogs belonging to one of the seven AKC groups (Working, Herding, Sporting, Non-sporting, Hounds, Terrier, and Toy). Naturally, Shih Tzu compete in the Toy Group. The AKC also offers children from 9 to 18 the opportunity to compete in junior showmanship events. Here, the juniors are judged on how well they present their dogs.

If you want to know more about conformation shows, you can start by joining a local kennel club that will have information on training classes for the show ring, or by contacting the AKC for more information. You should also attend a show as a visitor. If the grooming area is open to the public, talk to professional groomers to get some tips. If you are considering the purchase of a Shih Tzu, you will have the benefit of many expert breeders and exhibitors to talk to. Once you know what to expect, you can better enjoy the experience of competitive dog shows.

Good Citizen Test

The Good Citizen Test is an evaluation of the dog's ability and willingness to behave and act properly in public. This is the only AKC-sponsored activity that allows mixed-breed dogs to participate. Ten different tests are administered on a pass-fail basis. If you and your Shih Tzu pass all ten of the following tests, you can apply for the Canine Good Citizen certificate and collar tag.

- **Accepting a friendly stranger.** Your Shih Tzu must show no signs of aggression, shyness, or jealousy when approached by the evaluator. She must not break her position or jump on the evaluator, either.
- **Sitting politely for petting.** Your dog must sit still when approached and petted by the evaluator.
- **Appearance and grooming.** Your dog should calmly allow both grooming and hands-on examination by the evaluator. She is allowed to move during the test, but should not struggle.
- **Out for a walk.** Your pet should maneuver on a loose leash without pulling, struggling, or disobeying commands.
- **Walking through a crowd.** Your dog should be able to stay under control while walking in a public place with other people around.
- **Sitting and lying down.** Your Shih Tzu should act on command, and should remain in place until the evaluator instructs you to release her.
- **Coming when called.** This test determines if your dog will obediently come when called.
- **Reaction to other dogs.** Your dog will be tested on how she reacts to her peers. Grading will depend on her ability to remain calm and in control when other dogs are brought around.
- **Reaction to distractions.** Your dog must not be easily distracted by passing bicycles or joggers, or by sudden noises.
- **Supervised separation.** Your dog must be left alone with a stranger without becoming distraught.

HOW-TO: HOUSETRAINING

Let's face it: Housetraining a puppy is definitely not an activity that anyone really enjoys. But if you follow any of the three techniques described here, you will be able to speed up the process while avoiding many of the unwanted surprises.

Paper Training

The objective of paper training is to get your puppy to urinate and defecate on newspapers spread out in an area of your choosing. Naturally, you should choose an area that is easy to clean such as a kitchen or bathroom. Likewise, the area should not be too close to your puppy's eating or sleeping areas, because your Shih Tzu will instinctively try to keep those areas clean and will not excrete near them.

Begin by confining your puppy to the area you have chosen until she voids. If she used the paper, remove the top soiled sheet, and place fresh, clean papers under what were formerly the bottom sheets. By doing this, the scent from the newly exposed papers will be left so that the puppy can relocate the area (by smell) and repeat the act.

If the puppy misses the paper on her first attempt, get the scent of the dog's urine onto a sheet of newspaper and place it on top of the other sheets. Then thoroughly clean the area where the accident occurred. It is important to remove all scent from the inappropriate area that the puppy used so she will not become confused the next time she has to relieve herself.

After eating, drinking, playing, or waking up, your puppy will probably need to empty her bladder and bowels. Young puppies need to relieve themselves every few hours. Oftentimes, the only sign your puppy will give you is that she will begin sniffing the ground for the right place to do her duty. Some puppies may begin sniffing the ground and begin running around frantically, giving you only seconds to react. When this happens, pick up the puppy and place her on the paper in the designated area of your home. You can then gently restrain the puppy's movements until she has relieved herself on the paper.

Then remember the "fifth commandment," and praise your puppy for her efforts.

Crate Training

Crate training offers a faster and easier alternative to paper training, because it takes advantage of your puppy's instincts to keep its

A crate can help simplify training your Shih Tzu.

sleeping area clean. If your puppy is wary on her first encounter with the crate, make it more appealing by placing some toys inside. Establish a time frame for letting the puppy out of the crate. When it is time, take the puppy out of the crate and immediately bring her outdoors to relieve herself. If the puppy has an accident in the crate, confine her there with her excreta for about 30 minutes. By doing this, the puppy will quickly learn to restrain herself until you let her out of her crate. As your trust in the puppy grows and she adapts more to the schedule, you can let her out of her crate for longer periods. Eventually, you will be able to leave the crate door open at all times without fear of accidents, provided that you take your puppy outside as scheduled.

Outdoor Training

Outdoor training begins when you first bring your puppy home. Before taking her indoors, take her for a walk in the area you have chosen for her to eliminate in. Give your puppy plenty of time to do her duty, and praise her for a job well done. Verbal praise and petting will help build your puppy's confidence and will increase your chances of future successful performances.

Most puppies need to relieve themselves as many as six times a day, so you will need to take your puppy outdoors about once every three to four hours. It is also advisable to walk the puppy after each of her meals. When a puppy's stomach is full, she will exert additional pressure on the bladder, so it is best not to wait too long. You should take your puppy for her last walk as late in the evening as possible. This will give you the greatest chance that your Shih Tzu puppy will not suffer any accidents during the night. If you continue to bring your puppy to the same area each time and praise her for

each success, she will eventually seek out this area on her own.

Cleaning Up

Although it is true that canine droppings are aesthetically unpleasant, it is your responsibility as a dog owner to clean up after her. Because these droppings can be considered a minor health hazard, many towns and cities have made it illegal not to clean up after your pet.

Wherever you walk your Shih Tzu, carry a plastic bag or "pooper-scooper" with you and dispose of the mess in its proper place. When cleaning your garden or yard, pick up and dispose of the droppings in well-sealed plastic bags in a sealed garbage can instead of burying them underground, because roundworms and tapeworms can be transmitted in the feces. For those accidents that happen in the home, clean with an odor-eliminating disinfectant. Do not use ammonia because the smell may remind your puppy of her urine.

Accidents Will Happen

Regardless of which method of housetraining you choose, it is inevitable that accidents will occur. If you discover that while you were asleep your Shih Tzu puppy could no longer control herself, remember that it *was an accident.* It will not do you or your puppy any good to get angry or to administer punishment. Puppies have very short memories, so if you do not catch them in the act or make the discovery shortly afterward, a scolding will only confuse your pet. If you catch her in the act, rebuke your puppy with a sharp *"No!"* and then put her in her crate. Never spank your puppy and *never, never, never* put your puppy's nose in the mess. It is not only unsanitary, but it may also upset the puppy to such an extent that you will have a second mess to clean up.

INFORMATION

Kennel Clubs and Organizations

The American Kennel Club (AKC)
260 Madison Avenue
New York, NY 10016
Website: *www.akc.org*

The American Shih Tzu Club (ASTC)
279 Sun Valley Court
Ripon, CA 95366
Website: *www.americanshihtzuclub.org*
E-mail: *akotze@charter.net*

Orthopedic Foundation for Animals
2300 Nifong Boulevard
Columbia, MO 65201
Website: *www.offa.org*

Canine Eye Registration Foundation
South Campus Court, Building C
Purdue University
West Lafayette, IN 47907
Website: *www.vmdb.org/cerf.html*

The American Veterinary Medical Association
930 North Meacham Road
Schaumburg, IL 6017
Website: *www.avma.org*

Magazines

Dog Fancy
P.O. Box 6050
Mission Viejo, CA 92690
Website: *www.dogchannel.com/dfdc.portal.aspx*

Dogs Monthly
61 Great Whyte
Ramsey
Huntingdon
PE26 1HJ UK
Website: *www.dogsmonthly.co.uk*

Videos

Shih Tzu Around the World (from ASTC)
5136 36th Street West
Bradenton, FL 34210

Larson, Gregory and Tammarie. *The New Complete Shih Tzu Grooming Video* (1998). (E-mail: *lstalarson@aol.com*)

Useful Literature

Carlson, Delbert G., and James M. Giffin. *Dog Owner's Home Veterinary Handbook.* New York: Howell Book House (1992).

Cecil, Barbara, and Gerianne Darnell. *Competitive Obedience Training for the Small Dog.* Council Bluffs, IA: T9E Publishing (1994).

Dadds, Audrey. *The Shih Tzu.* Waterlooville, England: Kingdom Books (1995).

Forsyth, Jane and Robert. *Forsyth Guide to Successful Dog Showing.* New York: Howell Book House (1975).

Fox, Michael W. *Dog Body, Dog Mind: Exploring Canine Consciousness and Total Well Being.* Guilford, CT. The Lyons Press (2007).

Hogg, Peggy A., and Dr. Robert J. Berndt. *Grooming and Showing Toy Dogs.* Fairfax, VA. William Denlinger Co. (1976).

Joris, Victor. *The Complete Shih Tzu.* New York: Howell Book House (1994).

Kalstone, Shirlee. *How to Housebreak Your Dog in 7 Days.* New York: Bantam Books (2006).

Millan, Cesar, and Melissa Jo Peltier. *Be the Pack Leader: Use Cesar's Way to Transform Your Dog and Your Life.* New York: Crown (2007).

White, Jo Ann. *The Shih Tzu: Your Happy Healthy Pet.* Indianapolis, IN: Howell Book House (2005).

INDEX

Accessories, 25–27
Accidents happen, 91
American Kennel Club, 17, 19
Attack signs, 71, 72

Bad habits, 14, 43
Bathing, 38–39
Begging, 43, 81
Bleeding, 61–62
Boarding, 37
Body language, 71–72
Breed characteristics, 7–9
Breeders, 16–17, 37, 47
Broken bones, 61
Buying dog, 15–16

Cage, 33
Canine Eye Registry, 17
Children, 35–36
Choking, 28
Choosing
    adult or puppy?, 13–14
    considerations, 12
    good choice, 11–13
    male or female?, 14–15
Coat, 9, 17, 24, 38, 45, 48
Collar, 3, 26–27, 37, 80
Color, 17
Commands, 81–86
Communication, 72–73
Compact breed, 11
Competition, 88–89
Conformation events, 89
Constipation, 59
Crate, 22–23, 34, 36, 81
Curiosity, 74–75

Defecation, 33–34, 91
Dehydration, 37
Diarrhea, 48–49
Dog(s)
    biscuits, 39
    humans and, 5
    license, 19
    sitter, 37
Domestication, 70–71

Ears, 8, 39, 72
Elbow dysplasia, 17, 57, 59

Electrical wires, 31
Exercise, 24, 36, 47, 66
Expenses, 18–19
External parasites, 27
Eyes, 8, 17, 39, 55–56, 66, 72

Females, 14–15, 69
First Aid Kit, 62
Fleas, 52–53
Food, 37, 42–43, 45, 66
    calorie intake, 44
    dishes, 21, 25–26. 31
    number of meals, 44
    supplements, 44

Gait, 9
Good Citizen Tests, 89
Groomers, 47
Grooming, 19, 22, 31, 37–39, 59, 66
Gums, 39

Hazards, 35
Head, 8
Health disorders, 59–61
Heatstroke, 44
Hereditary ailments, 17, 55–56
Hindquarters, 9
Hip dysplasia, 17, 56–57
Housetraining, 22, 90–91
Hurdle jumping, 87–88

ID tag, 27, 36
Illness symptoms, 48
Immune system, 49–50, 75
Immunization, 19, 49–50
Indoor needs, 21–24
Infectious diseases, 50–51, 54
Information, 92–93
Instinctive behavior, 69–70, 28, 77

Leash, 26–27, 31, 33, 37, 80
Lice, 54
Loneliness, 32–34
Longevity, 63, 72

Males, 14–15, 69
Medications, 65
Mites, 54–55
Motion-sickness, 37
Muzzle, 27, 37, 60

Neck and nose, 8
Neutering, 15
Normal physiologic values, 63
Nutrition, 41–43, 45, 47

Obedience school, 84–85
Object relinquishing, 86–87
Older dogs, 44, 63–66, 75
Outdoors, 24

Pack leader, 77
Parasites
    external, 52–55
    internal, 51–52
Paws, 39
Pedigree, 17
Pet sitters, 37, 47
Play, 22
Poisoning, 62–63
Praise, 80, 91
Puppy
    alone, 80–81
    eating, 33
    feeding, 33, 44
    in home, 18, 32–35
    life changes, 74–75
    lifting and carrying, 35
    proofing, 31, 81
    safety rules, 22
    selecting, 17
    sitting, 35
    sleeping, 33–34
    training, 33, 77–79

Ranking order, 69, 71, 77
Reflective tape, 27
Rescue organization, 14
Retrieving, 87

Saying good-bye, 66–67
Scent marking, 69–71
Sense organs, 72

Sexual maturity, 75
Shih Tzu Club of America, 19
Shih Tzu origins, 5
Shock, 61
Show dog, 17
Size, 8
Skeletal disorders, 56–57, 59
Sleeping, 34
    area, 22, 65
    box, 23–24, 33, 81
Spayed, 15

Table scraps, 43–44
Tail, 8
Tapeworm, 51
Teeth, 39, 66
Temperament, 9, 11, 14, 17, 22, 44, 63, 71
Temperature, 36, 63
Ticks, 27, 53–54
Toys, 27–29, 28, 31, 34
Training
    crate, 90–91
    obedience, 84
    outdoor, 91
    paper, 90
    problems, 88
    puppy, 33, 77–79
    treats and, 79–80
Travel, 36–37
Travel crate, 22

Urination, 33–34, 91

Vacation time, 36–37
Vaccination records, 17
Vaccines, 50–51
Veterinarian, 17, 27, 37, 41, 45, 47–49, 66
Veterinary costs, 19
Vomiting, 48

Water, 21, 25–26, 31, 37, 44
Weight, 35, 45
Whimpering, 48, 71
Whining, 34, 66, 71
Worms, 51–52

About the Author

Jaime J. Sucher is Director of Research and Development for a manufacturer of pet products. He has written numerous articles on pet nutrition, and is the author of *Shetland Sheepdogs* and *Golden Retrievers*.

Photo Credits

Barbara Augello: page 73; Norvia Behling: pages 15, 23, 76; Seth Casteel: pages 10, 20, 32, 47, 50, 58, 83; Kent Dannen: page 18; Tara Darling: page 6; Shirley Fernandez: page 64; Sharon Eide Elizabeth Flynn: pages 19, 21, 31, 34, 67; Jeanmfogle.com: pages 53, 74; Paulette Johnson: pages 42, 45, 49, 84; Pets by Paulette: pages 4, 11, 41, 57, 69, 77, 90; Shutterstock: pages 2–3, 5, 9, 13, 16, 28, 30, 35, 36, 40, 63, 68, 75, 82, 86, 92, 93; Kira Stackhouse: pages 24, 70; Connie Summers: pages 25, 26, 29, 37, 38, 39, 46, 79, 80.

Cover Photos

Shutterstock: front cover, back cover, inside front cover, inside back cover.

Important Note

This book is concerned with selecting, keeping, and raising Shih Tzu. The publisher and the author think it is important to point out that the advice and information for Shih Tzu maintenance applies to healthy, normally developed animals. Anyone who acquires an adult dog or one from an animal shelter must consider that the animal may have behavioral problems and may, for example, bite without any visible provocation. Anxiety-biters are dangerous for the owner as well as the general public.

Caution is further advised in the association of children with dogs, in meetings with other dogs, and in exercising the dog without a leash.

A Note About Pronouns

Many dog lovers feel that the pronoun "it" is not appropriate when referring to a pet that can be such a wonderful part of our lives. For this reason, Shih Tzu are described as "she" throughout this book unless the topic specifically relates to male dogs. This by no means infers any preference, nor should it be taken as an indication that either sex is particularly problematic.

© Copyright 2010, 2000, 1991 by Barron's Educational Series, Inc.

All rights reserved.
No part of this publication may be reproduced or distributed in any form or by any means without the written permission of the copyright owner.

All inquiries should be addressed to:
Barron's Educational Series, Inc.
250 Wireless Boulevard
Hauppauge, NY 11788
www.barronseduc.com

Library of Congress Catalog Card No. 2010010640

ISBN-13: 978-0-7641-4352-6
ISBN-10: 0-7641-4352-2

Library of Congress Cataloging-in-Publication Data
Sucher, Jaime J.
Shih tzu : everything about purchase, housing, care, nutrition, and health care / Jaime Sucher ; illustrations by Michele Earle-Bridges.
p. cm.
Includes index.
ISBN-13: 978-0-7641-4352-6
ISBN-10: 0-7641-4352-2
1. Shih tzu. I. Title.
SF429.S64S83 2010
636.76—dc22   2010010640

Printed in China

9 8 7 6 5 4 3 2 1